THE ROOFED GRAVES
OF DELMARVA

THE ROOFED GRAVES OF DELMARVA

CHRISTOPHER SLAVENS

Bald Cypress Books
Laurel, Delaware

baldcypressbooks.com

Copyright © 2020, 2025 by Christopher Slavens.
All rights reserved.

ISBN: 978-0-578-63663-4
Library of Congress Control Number: 2020900827

Publisher's Cataloging-in-Publication Data

Slavens, Christopher, author.
The Roofed Graves of Delmarva / Christopher Slavens.
Second trade paperback edition.
Laurel, DE: Bald Cypress Books, 2020.
LCCN: 2020900827 | ISBN: 978-0-578-63663-4
Sepulchral monuments—Delmarva Peninsula.
Delmarva Peninsula—Social life and customs.
Delmarva Peninsula—History.
Cemeteries—Delaware—Sussex County.
Cemeteries—Maryland—Wicomico County.

Front cover images: Bethel Methodist Episcopal Church (top) and a roofed grave at Bethel (bottom), photographed by Frank R. Zebley. Courtesy of the Delaware Public Archives.

Back cover images: Roofed grave at Daisey Cemetery (top). Courtesy of Kathy McGill. Roofed grave at King's Church (bottom), photographed by Frank R. Zebley. Courtesy of the Delaware Public Archives.

This is a print-on-demand book. The production process may result in variations between individual copies.

Published in the United States of America

Although many people contributed to this research project in one way or another, a few are especially deserving of my gratitude: Ned & Norma Jean Fowler, for their feedback and encouragement; Jim Hall, for his interest, enthusiasm, and assistance; Ric Finch, for corresponding with me and mentioning my research in his wonderful paper about comb graves; Jim Bowden, who sent me two of the earliest articles about roofed graves; and Tom Slavens, my father, who read early drafts and caught several errors I had overlooked.

Most of all, I thank Crystal, my wife, for sharing (or putting up with) my love of old graveyards. She braved briars and mosquitoes on many summer afternoons as we searched local cemeteries for evidence of roofed graves, and she assisted with research, proofreading, and book design. This book would not have been completed without her support.

CONTENTS

I.	Roofed Graves in Primary Sources	1
II.	The Roofs	13
III.	Bethel M. E. Church	19
IV.	The West Cemetery & King's M. E. Church	29
V.	Three More Sussex Cemeteries	37
VI.	Roofed Graves in Wicomico County	43
VII.	Dating the Roofed Grave Custom	49
VIII.	Comb Graves & Grave Shelters	55
IX.	An American Indian Connection?	65
X.	More Questions Than Answers	80

Notes

CHAPTER I

ROOFED GRAVES IN PRIMARY SOURCES

A curious article appeared in the *Binghamton Press*, a New York newspaper, in the spring of 1932:

> *200-Year-Old Cemetery Has Roofed Graves*
>
> *Berlin, Md., March 24—(United Press)—The quaintest cemetery in the United States is located on the Mason-Dixon line, at Bethel Church, northwest of Whaleyville, near here. Peaked shingle built roofs instead of imposing marble monuments mark the graves. This unique cemetery is thought to be about 200 years old.*
>
> *As if to protect those buried there some one, decades ago, constructed peaked shingle roofs over the graves. These shelters are about three feet high in the middle, the sides touching the ground. Built of cypress wood and shingles these roofs run the length of the graves forming their only*

location, as no mounds are visible. Some of the lumber has rotted by this time, but the form and general shape of this "village of the dead" still remain.[1]

The piece appeared in more than a dozen papers across the nation. Locally, a more detailed article appeared in Wilmington's *Every Evening* on April 13, 1932:

Roofed graves in Bethel cemetery, near Berlin, Md., show that the shingles of the old days withstood storm and sunshine more than two centuries, and while, at last, showing the ravages wrought by the elements, some are still well preserved. The custom doubtless was imported with some of the people who came from the Old World, and expresses a deep regard for the welfare of the bodies of their kindred. The roofs run into sharp peaks, three feet high and slope to the ground, so neither rain nor snow can disturb the repose of the sleepers.

The cypress shingles recall that many houses in lower Delaware were built of similar material taken from one of the major swamps in Sussex county and that the wood is regarded as almost indestructible after having lain for decades under water.

The ancient Maryland graveyard is a survival of the earliest settlers in that section and the roofed graves reflect the veneration and love bestowed upon the dead. Perhaps those bodies laid in the ancient cemetery were covered against the weather with the expectation that the remains would eventually be taken back to the Old World for final burial. Such provision for the dead perhaps bespeaks the profound sorrow for the passing of kindred that was awakened in the early days, and manifests the tender care exercised in providing repose for the ashes where they would not be harmed by the elements of nature, and could be reclaimed.[2]

And so it was that Bethel Methodist Episcopal Church and its scattered cemetery plots, located south of Gumboro at a quiet, dusty intersection on the outskirts of the Pocomoke Swamp, briefly emerged from obscurity and attracted the curiosity of the outside world. These are the earliest known descriptions of its peculiar roofed graves, though it is possible that earlier references lurk in overlooked sources. Despite a few errors—the site is located on the Transpeninsular Line, not the Mason-Dixon Line; most of the graves are located north of the line, in Delaware; and it is very doubtful that they date back to the 1730s—the articles serve as a good introduction to the roofed grave custom, offering approximate measurements, materials, and theories about age, origins, and purpose.

The graves at Bethel were mentioned again in *Delaware: A Guide to the First State*, compiled by members of the Federal Writers Project and published in 1938. Following a lengthy section about the Great Pocomoke Swamp and its shingle-making industry, readers were guided to the church, where:

> *On the wooded north bank of the road, west of the building, are several old graves with shingle roofs, almost hidden by undergrowth. They are the only remaining examples of the once-popular local custom of placing a small pitched roof over a grave to keep off the rain. Some of the old graveyards in this section have cypress slabs instead of gravestones.*[3]

Apparently the roofed graves were the sole reason for mentioning the church, because the writer offered no additional information about it.

Bethel M. E. Church before 1941; note the overgrown cemetery area to the left. Photo by Frank R. Zebley. *Courtesy of the Delaware Public Archives.*

At about this time, Frank R. Zebley, a Wilmington builder, writer, and politician, was researching the history of churches in Delaware, and visited Bethel. He was fascinated by the roofed graves, writing:

> *In the old graveyard a few roofed-over graves can be seen, one of the few places in Delaware where any of these graves remain. These roofs are A shaped with the gables closed in, rest directly on the ground with the entire frame-work covered with shingles. One can only conjecture as to the reason the graves of a century ago were so covered yet when one considers how shallow the graves were dug at that time it is not surprising that sensitive persons felt the need of added protection for the bodies of their loved ones.*
>
> *The writer is convinced that these roofs were for protection, and not, as some persons claim, grave markers*

erected by persons who could not afford a tombstone. In proof of this, in the private graveyard on the farm of Ira West, near Trussum Pond, there are several graves over which roofs have been built and each one of these graves has both a headstone and a footstone. The most recent of these were over the graves of John C. West who died in 1858 and Mahala West who died in 1852.[4]

Additionally, in Zebley's history of King's M. E. Church, located near Trussum Pond, he noted, "The tombstones date back to 1857. There is one roofed-over grave."[5] The final result of Zebley's research was *The Churches of Delaware*, published in 1947 with a photograph of one of the roofed graves at Bethel. The Delaware Public Archives holds additional photographs taken at the site, including two of roofed graves, as well as a photograph of the roofed grave at King's.

Roofed grave at Bethel M. E. Church, photographed by Frank R. Zebley. *Courtesy of the Delaware Public Archives.*

During the twelve-year period of Zebley's research, the *Journal-Every Evening* published two articles about the site, the first of which featured a photograph which might pre-date Zebley's. Entitled "Curious and Forgotten Graves Lure Camera Hobbyist Along Delmarva Peninsula By-Ways," the article published on April 19, 1941, chronicled Wilmington resident C. Stayton Jones' hobby of visiting and photographing historic or unusual sites, particularly cemeteries.[6]

> *He gets his information from old books, tips from travelers and from natives of the localities. For example—the roof covered graves, near Gumboro, tucked away in a lonely grass plot . . .*
>
> *. . . "While I was searching for these graves, I met an old native of Sussex County who said he had cut wood for such memorials in his youth," Jones recalled.*

A photograph of three roofed graves, presumably taken by Jones, was printed with the article. The photograph is undated, but the fact that he was aware of the graves at Bethel and searched for them suggests that he learned of their existence from an early source, possibly the Delaware Guide, and visited the site in the 1930s.

On November 11, 1941, the *Journal-Every Evening* published a much more colorful piece about the graves at Bethel by Berlin resident Jack Culver.[7] Some of his statements about the history of the site are questionable, but the account is rich in detail:

> *Whispering pines and sighing cypress today have all but hidden from view the ancient cemetery near Bethel church. Here and there, beneath the carpet of pine needles*

and leaves on the forest floor, one might uncover pieces of rotted board or a piece of weather beaten cypress shingle, mute evidence of the final resting places of the early residents of Bethel . . .

. . . Visitors to the fascinating spot, however, might venture through a veritable growth of briars and underbrush for a considerable distance before they find one of the several peaked roof covered graves still intact.

The old cemetery at Bethel antedates Bethel Church itself, whose walls were sheathed with Pocomoke cypress swamp shingles, hewn out by hand, back in 1840.

The entire text of Culver's article is included in Chapter III, along with his photograph of one of the roofed graves. His claim that the site was used as a cemetery before 1840 is explored further in Chapters IV and VII.

Following the flurry of interest in roofed graves in the 1930s–1940s, they were written about only occasionally, and in lesser detail. The early sources inspired no academic studies, which is unfortunate, because none of the roofs described by the aforementioned sources have survived to the present. It is assumed that the last remaining examples were deliberately removed by caretakers due to their deteriorating condition.

Roofed Graves in Wicomico County

Sometime prior to 1964, the late John E. Jacob, Jr., a Salisbury attorney who served as president of the Wicomico Historical Society and wrote several books about local history, began visiting cemeteries in Wicomico County and transcribing the inscriptions found on grave markers, focusing on those dating to the eighteenth and nineteenth centuries. In an article entitled "Who Are These Below? Grave Hunter Collects Names From Old Wicomico Markers," published by the *Daily Times* on December 5, 1964, Dick Moore reported that Jacob had recorded more than six thousand inscriptions.[8] He went on to say:

> *In colonial times and even up to the Civil War era, stones for marking graves were a luxury a few could afford in this part of the country. Wooden markers soon rotted away, as did a wooden lean-to arrangement which people put over graves in the last century.*

A few weeks later, Jacob gave a talk about his project to the Quota Club of the Eastern Shore. A brief article about the event mentioned "the shingle dog-house roof" among other forms of grave markers.[9]

In 1966, the *Daily Times* triumphantly summarized Jacob's research in an article entitled "Salisbury Attorney's Hunt For Graves Is Over."[10] Author Orlando V. Wootten reported:

> *Mr. Jacob found recently a type of grave marker that he had often heard about, but could never find until Grant Powell, forester for the E. S. Adkins Co., located three deep in the woods on the Winder Layfield farm off the Mary Downing Road. These were little shingle roofs built over the graves. The farm itself is in a remote clearing and the graveyard even farther in.*
>
> *Mr. Layfield, himself 74, said that the graves were those of his grandparents, and that the rotting structures could be 120 years old. Mr. Layfield said that he did not know why they were built, but Mr. Jacob thought that they were erected out of sentimental respect for the*

dead, to keep off the rain, and to protect the graves from animals. They are found only in the eastern part of the county, Mr. Jacob said, *and contain no marking as to who lies below.*

An accompanying photograph is the only known photograph of a roofed grave in Wicomico County. The caption describes the structure as "typical of many once found in the eastern part of the county. It is the only good one Mr. Jacob has ever seen."

Jacob's research was published in the form of a book in 1971. In his introduction to *Graveyards and Gravestones of Wicomico*, he explained that wooden grave markers were popular in the early nineteenth century due to the lack of local sources of stone and the cost of imported stone markers, and that local demand for stone markers did not support a stonecutter in nearby Salisbury until about 1850.[11] He also noted:

> *One type of marker requires special mention, the roof. It was the custom in the eastern section of Wicomico for many years to build a roof over a new grave. The roof was built on an 'A' frame, the peak about thirty inches high, with the structure covering the entire grave. The last one standing in Wicomico County is shown on page 11. This one was erected at least a hundred years ago according to information from a member of the family.*
>
> *Diligent inquiry about the origin of the custom has produced no satisfactory answers. Some people claim they were erected to keep pigs and wild animals from rooting up the bodies. Others have told me they were built to keep people and animals off the graves until the mortar in the shallow arches of the brick vaults had hardened. Neither of these explanations tells the whole story. I believe the*

custom originated because the families of the deceased felt that the primitive facilities of the time required them to afford the bodies of their loved ones more protection from the seepage of rain and snow into the earth.

Unfortunately, the promised photograph is absent from the book, but it is assumed that it was the same photograph published by the *Daily Times* in 1966.

More Sites in Sussex County

Amidst the revival of public interest in community history that accompanied the bicentennial celebration in 1976, brief references to roofed graves found their way into three books about Sussex County. Two, *Visiting Sussex: Even If You Live Here* by Robert H. Robinson, and *The History of Sussex County* by Dick Carter, briefly mentioned roofs at previously known sites. Carter used the Delaware Guide as a source,[12] and it is assumed that Robinson, who passed away in 2017, did the same. The third book, *Folklore of Sussex County, Delaware*, by Dorothy W. Pepper, identified a fourth specific site in Sussex County:

> *Roofed-Over Graves*
> *An old graveyard in back of Millard Johnson's home near Bayard had some graves with a roof on top of each one. The A-shaped roofs were made of cedar shingles pointed on top exactly like a house roof, and each one covered an entire grave. Some were known to exist in the Bethel Methodist Church graveyard south of Gumboro. Few old roofed-over graves remain today in Delaware.*[13]

The cemetery in question is the Daisey Cemetery (see Chapter IV), which is located near the intersection of Wilgus Cemetery Road and Honeysuckle Road between Roxana and Bayard, and is known to have featured at least one roof as recently as 1947.[14] Although Pepper implied that the structures at both the Bayard and Bethel sites were no longer there, it is interesting that she also implied that some still survived elsewhere in Delaware as recently as 1976.

A fifth site in Sussex County was identified in 2016 by Laurel resident Kendal Jones, who recalls visiting a small plot associated with the Timmons family near Lowe's Crossroads as a boy in the early to mid-1930s, and seeing a couple of small A-framed, shingled roofs. By the 1950s, all that remained were fragments of wood under the leaves.[15]

Following the publication of the first edition of this book in 2020, a Laurel man reported having seen roofed graves while hunting north of Lowe's Crossroads years earlier, but the location of this cemetery is unknown.[16]

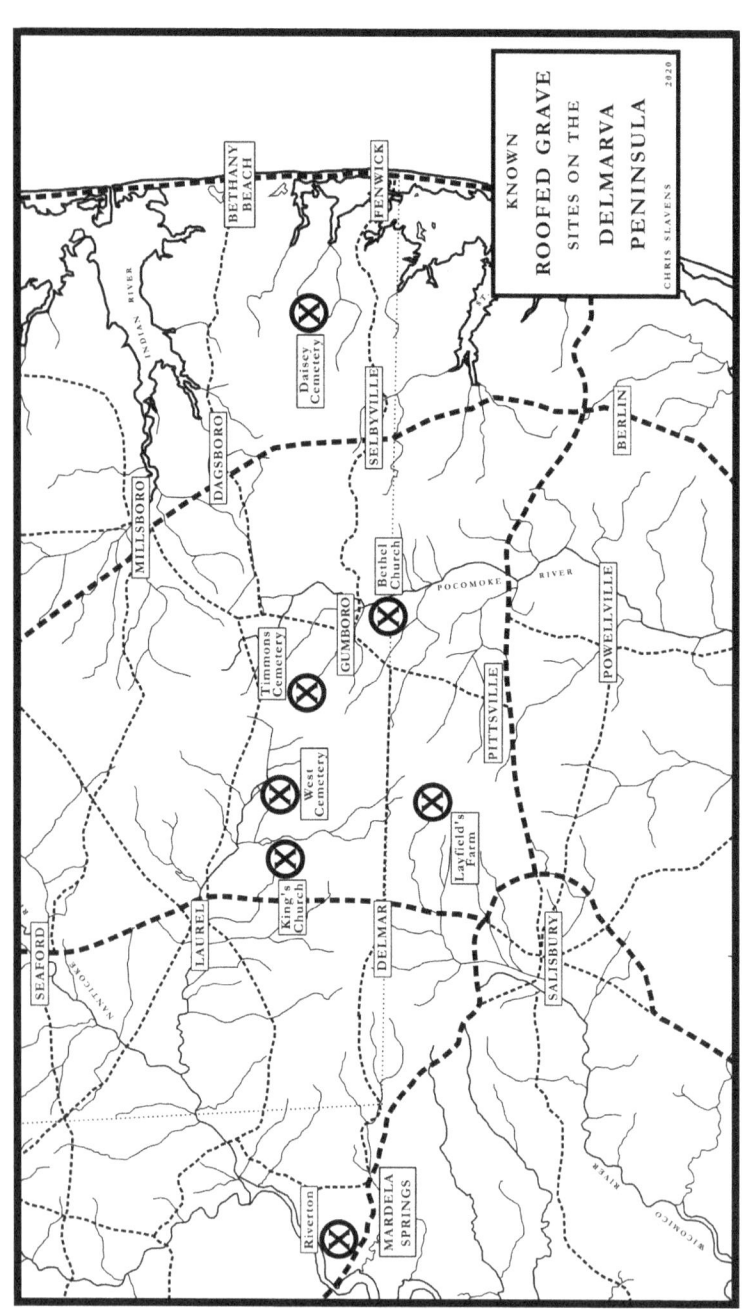

CHAPTER II

THE ROOFS

No roofed graves are known to survive on the Delmarva Peninsula,[1] although it is tantalizingly possible that some are still rotting away in forgotten, overgrown plots, perhaps deep in the woods, visited only by wildlife. In the absence of a physical roof to study, photographs and eyewitness accounts are the next best thing.

The available evidence suggests that roofs at different sites were remarkably similar. The typical roof was long enough to cover an entire grave, approximately thirty to thirty-six inches tall at the peak, gabled at the ends, covered with bald cypress or cedar shingles, and placed directly on the ground. It is probable that the roof's height depended on its length, which was determined by the height of the deceased; the roof over little Elijah Daisey's grave in the Daisey Cemetery was visibly smaller.

It is important to note that the structures were literal,

functional, shingled roofs, probably made of the same shingles used to shelter homes, outhouses, corn cribs, and the like. Additionally, most of the known sites are located within a few miles of the Pocomoke or Cypress Swamp, the source of ancient, rot-resistant bald cypress lumber. The local shingle-making industry, and the durability of its products, were described by the Federal Writers Project:

> *Men with holly-wood mauls and heavy iron blades called 'frows' rived the cypress cylinders into shingle blocks and then draw-knifed them into the 30-inch shingles that would wear out but never decay. Nearly all the mossy old houses of southeastern Delaware and nearby Maryland are sheathed with these lustrous hand-riven Pocomoke cypress shingles. Some have worn as thin as cardboard after 150 years of weather, but are still as sound as the day they were nailed on hand-hewn oak joists. Since the first drainage ditches were dug through the swamp in 1867 there have been successive peat fires, but the fire of 1930 put an end to all shingle-making . . .*[2]

Although it is clear that the shingles used for the roofs were quite durable and could have survived for a century or longer, the durability of the structures as a whole would have depended on the type of lumber used in the construction of their frames, which were in direct contact with the ground and therefore exposed to moisture as well as wood-destroying insects. Bald cypress or cedar frames would have survived much longer than, say, oak, but even they would inevitably succumb to the elements, given enough time, which is probably the primary reason that the structures have not survived to the present. The absence of any fragments at the known sites suggests that deliberate removal was also a factor.

A roof in poor condition at the Bethel site, photographed by Frank R. Zebley, probably in 1941. *Courtesy of the Delaware Public Archives.*

But why build a functional roof over a grave? The Delmarva Peninsula is home to other interesting grave markers including wooden headboards, hand-inscribed cement slabs, and a pair of millstones, but they merely mark the locations of the graves beneath them. The roofs, on the other hand, served not only as markers, but also as shelters. Jacob mentioned that some people thought "they were built to keep people and animals off the graves until the mortar in the shallow arches of the brick vaults had hardened," but he believed they were intended to shelter the graves and their contents from rain and snow.[3] A similar statement appears in *Delaware: A Guide to the First State*. If the latter theory is correct, one still wonders why people in the past would have felt the need to shield a grave from rain.

Vague traditions and superstitions involving graves and weather have been noted by many writers. In the Northeast, rain falling into an open grave signaled that there would be another burial in the same cemetery in three days, while rain falling onto a "new-made grave" meant that a relative of the deceased would die within one year.[4]

The Frank C. Brown Collection of NC Folklore includes several pages of superstitions concerning graves and funerals, many of them involving rain. Some of them seem to be contradictory—for example, "Blessed is the corpse that the rain falls on," yet, "It is bad luck for rain to fall into a grave"—but several distinct traditions maintain that rain falling into an open grave foreshadowed another death anywhere from the very next day to the end of the year.[5] A grave shelter might have allowed mourners to honor both traditions, enjoying the supposed good luck associated with a rainy funeral, while keeping the grave itself rain-free.

A similar superstition may have existed among the French Acadians of Louisiana, where:

> *Once upon a time an aged Acadian lay upon his deathbed. He called his grieving sons and daughters to his side and made known his last wishes. "My children," he said, "bury me in the corner pasture by the big oak trees. And don't let the rain fall on my face." With that he made the sign of the cross and breathed his last. The old man was laid out in a homemade coffin in the simple fashion of the time, and buried in a grave dug at the spot he had indicated. This fulfilled only part of his request: his dutiful children held a family counsel and decided that the best way to keep the rain from falling on papa's face was to build a house over his grave.*[6]

The tradition also existed in Mississippi, as a 1986 newspaper article about "covered graves" reported:

> *Mrs. G. C. Ross of Jackson remembers those graves with little wooden houses built over them. The wooden covers were not sturdy structures, usually open immediately*

under the roof and then enclosed at a level of two or three feet.

As her grandfather had said, "I don't want it to rain on me." That was the reason for these covers.[7]

In 2016, two elderly Sussex Countians—one a man living on the east side of the swamp near Frankford; the other a lady living near Omar—recalled that older relatives had requested that their graves be covered with concrete or cement because they didn't want to have dirt on top of them.[8] This unusual, unexplained request isn't necessarily connected to the roofed grave tradition, but it illustrates how some people were concerned about the treatment of their remains in years gone by.

On a practical level, a roof may have prevented the soil below from collapsing into the grave, a real possibility in the days when a grave consisted only of a simple wooden coffin in the ground. It also would have prevented passersby from walking on the grave. Today this act is widely regarded as being mildly disrespectful, but in the days before the widespread use of burial vaults, it could have resulted in the careless walker sinking through soft soil and into the grave. Shingled roofs may be considered a wooden alternative to ledger stones, box graves, concrete slabs, and the exposed burial vault (which is more common in the flood-prone communities of the lower peninsula, but occasionally found within the roofed grave range), all of which cover an entire grave and offer some degree of protection.

In short, the true purpose of the roofed graves of Delmarva remains a matter of speculation.

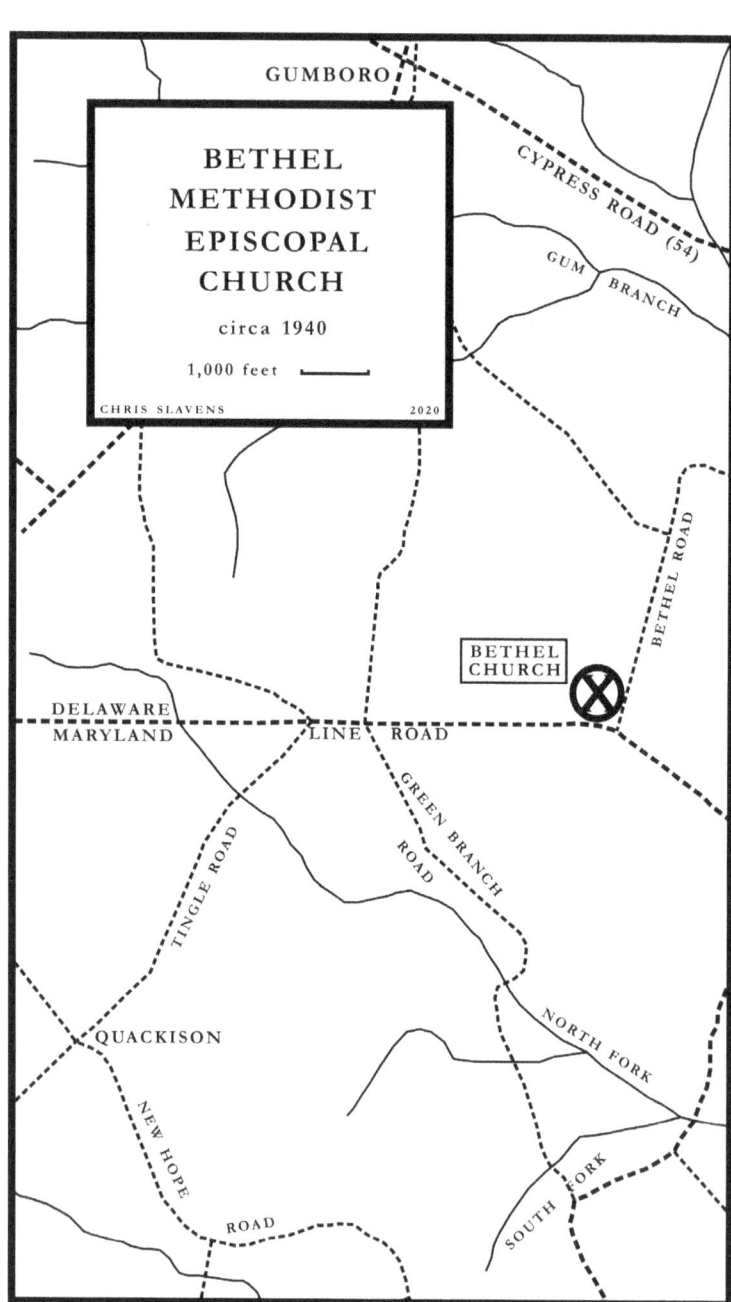

CHAPTER III

BETHEL M. E. CHURCH

Bethel United Methodist Church, formerly Bethel Methodist Episcopal Church, stands on a low hill at the intersection of Line Road and Bethel Road, just north of the Transpeninsular Line, which divides Sussex County, Delaware, and Wicomico County, Maryland. There are several scattered cemetery plots containing, perhaps, a couple of hundred graves; some new and well-kept, many swallowed by thick vines, briars, and sassafras. For this reason, some of the graves are more accessible during the winter, though the peaceful site is beautiful during the spring and summer.

Many of the oldest graves are not marked at all. The area between the church and the "north bank" of Line Road mentioned by the Federal Writers Project in 1938, and said to be overgrown by Culver in 1941, is now a well-tended lawn broken only by the occasional leaning headstone. A second area of interest is located just south of Line Road and appears, at first glance, to be an impenetrable mass of bushes and briars, but in fact there are several old cement headstones there, including that of Isaac Hall. It is possible that these two areas, which seem like separate plots today, make up the original cemetery, and the public road developed as a lane through its center.

Jack Culver's article, published in 1941, offers the earliest history of the site, though some of his claims are questionable:

Peaked Cypress Shingle Crypts
Cover Ancient Worcester Graves

SNOW HILL, Md., Nov. 11—(Special)—Twenty miles north of this Worcester County seat, bordering the Mason-Dixon line, and the great swamp at the headwaters of the Pocomoke River is perhaps the strangest looking cemetery to be found on the Delaware peninsula today.

For instead of the conventional tombstone or marble monument, the ancient graves therein are covered by peaked roofs, sheathed with weather-worn Pocomoke swamp cypress shingles.

This ancient cemetery adjoins one of lower Delaware's oldest churches, Bethel Methodist, located on the Maryland-Delaware boundary, six miles north of Willards, Md.

Whispering pines and sighing cypress today have all but hidden from view the ancient cemetery near Bethel church. Here and there, beneath the carpet of pine needles and leaves on the forest floor, one might uncover pieces of rotted board or a piece of weather beaten cypress shingle, mute evidence of the final resting places of the early residents of Bethel.

Roofed grave at Bethel M. E. Church, photographed by Jack Culver. The *Daily Times*, November 11, 1941.

Visitors to the fascinating spot, however, might venture through a veritable growth of briars and underbrush for a considerable distance before they find one of the several peaked roof covered graves still intact.

The old cemetery at Bethel antedates Bethel Church itself, whose walls were sheathed with Pocomoke cypress swamp shingles, hewn out by hand, back in 1840.

No one knows just when the first person was buried in the ancient churchyard, nor when the first peaked roof of cypress shingles was built as a cover over the graves of early settlers found there.

Not even Thomas J. Ake, 86-year-old lifelong resident of Bethel section, can supply any information as to the true age of the ancient cemetery.

Mr. Ake is certain however, that the peaked roofs

of cypress shingles were not placed above the graves as protection against wild bears that once roamed the great cypress swamp nearby. Instead, he says, the graves were covered by roofs as a mark of respect and in early days took the place of tombstone markers, then hard to obtain in this section of the shore.

It has been well over 150 years since the last peaked roof was built over any grave in the cemetery, Mr. Ake declares, basing his deduction on stories handed down to him by his father and grandfather.

Long before 1840, when the present Bethel church was built, the site was a noted camp meeting place, records show. Methodist meetings were held in an earlier church there. The last annual camp meeting was held at Bethel in 1917.

The cypress shingled peaked roofs that still cover several graves in old Bethel cemetery are worn thin by the elements. They wear out in time, but they never decay. It is this sheathing that gives these grave markers their gray lustre by day and their long, soft lavender shadows at sunset.

The Rev. Ward Mills of Gumboro, Del., conducts Sunday afternoon service in old Bethel Methodist Church now. His congregation numbers many whose ancestors sleep the sleep of the dead beneath the peaked cypress shingled roofs in the old cemetery nearby.[1]

Zebley's history of the church, published in *The Churches of Delaware* in 1947, contradicts Culver's on several points:

Bethel Methodist Church (M.E.) is located on the Line Road south of Gumboro. It was built in 1841 on a site purchased on Feb. 23, 1841 from Jos. S. Barnard.

The first services were held on February 23 of that year. The church was rebuilt in 1892 when the two doors were replaced by one door. The interior fittings are the same as originally built. In 1941, the old camp-meeting tabernacle was converted into a social-hall. In the old graveyard a few roofed-over graves can be seen, one of the few places in Delaware where any of these graves remain. These roofs are A shaped with the gables closed in, rest directly on the ground with the entire frame-work covered with shingles. One can only conjecture as to the reason the graves of a century ago were so covered yet when one considers how shallow the graves were dug at that time it is not surprising that sensitive persons felt the need of added protection for the bodies of their loved ones.

The writer is convinced that these roofs were for protection and not, as some persons claim, grave markers erected by persons who could not afford a tombstone.[2]

Roofed graves at Bethel, photographed by Frank R. Zebley. *Courtesy of the Delaware Public Archives.*

Therefore, the site's early history is disputed. Zebley reported that the original church was built in 1841, and referred to the roofed graves as "the graves of a century ago" despite the absence of headstones, perhaps assuming they dated to the church's earliest years. Yet Culver reported that an earlier structure built at an unknown date was replaced in 1840, and that the cemetery predates the church. Additionally, his local source, 86-year-old Thomas J. Ake, claimed that the roofed graves were more than 150 years old in 1941, implying a date of 1790 or earlier. Ake vaguely cited "stories handed down to him by his father and grandfather."

Ake's father, John S. Ake, lived 1829-1880, and is buried at Bethel. His grandfather, Thomas D. Ake, was born circa 1798 according to the 1850 census. Both men would have been familiar with the early history of the site; the question is whether Thomas J. Ake's claim that the roofed graves date back to 1790 or earlier is accurate. Although it should not be dismissed lightly, the available evidence does not seem to support it.

Also in 1941, C. Stayton Jones reported that an old local resident remembered cutting wood for roofed graves in his youth;[3] although the man's identity and age are unknown, it is reasonable to assume that he must have been born during the mid- to late nineteenth century. This is more consistent with Zebley's estimate of the graves' age and the known history of the site. Still, the roofs standing in the 1930s–1940s were not the only ones ever built at the site. The early accounts and photographs make it clear that the condition of the surviving roofs varied greatly, and they were surrounded by fragments of shingles and boards, the last remnants of older roofs. This suggests that the custom was practiced over an extended period of time. The important question of the age and origins of not only the handful of roofs which survived into the twentieth century, but also the custom as a whole, is explored further in Chapter VII.

As for the existence of a church prior to the 1840s, no evidence exists to support this claim, and the limited available evidence weighs against it. According to Zebley, the church "was built in 1841 on a site purchased on Feb. 23, 1841 from Jos. S. Barnard. The first services were held on February 23 of that year." The deed of sale, dated February 23, 1841, describes the parcel as "containing one half acre more or less whereon is now erected a Meeting house called the Bethel Meeting House…"[4] The site is almost certainly part of an enormous, 4,218.5-acre parcel which spanned the boundaries between Dagsborough, Broad Creek, and Baltimore Hundreds when Barnard acquired it on December 13, 1840.[5] This deed does not mention a meeting house, cemetery, or any other structure. However, it is quite possible that camp meetings were held at the site prior to the construction of the church. Perhaps future research will turn up more information about the site's history.

Despite the errors in Culver's article, the absence of evidence for a church building predating the one built in 1841, and the reasonable conclusion that Ake was mistaken about the age of the roofed graves there, one should not ignore the possibility that the site was used as a cemetery prior to the church's construction. Its relatively high elevation in comparison with the surrounding land at the edge of the swamp would have made it an ideal site even prior to the construction of a house of worship. Furthermore, aerial photographs taken in 1937 and 1954 suggest that some of the old graves on the north side of Line Road were in a small clearing of their own, yet separated from the church by a wooded or overgrown patch. This visible yet unexplained separation could indicate that the oldest graves were not always associated with the church, but there simply is not enough evidence to support such a conclusion.

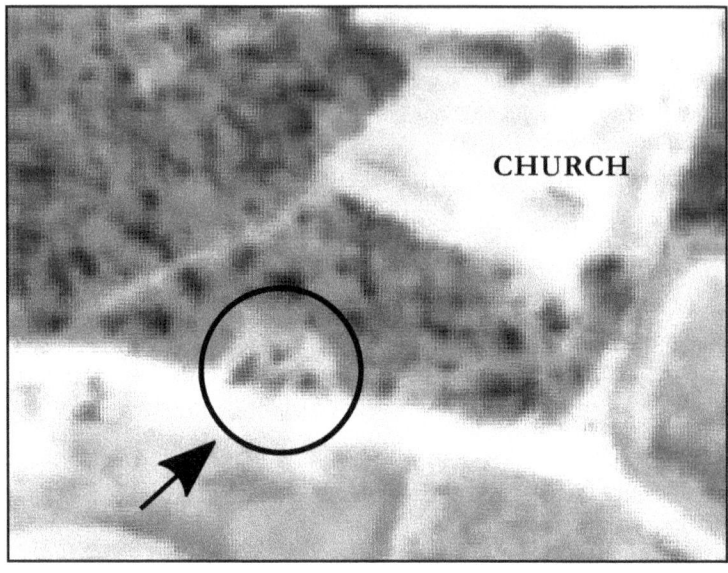

Enhanced aerial photograph of the Bethel site, 1954. Note the partially cleared area on the north side of Line Road.

For the sake of thoroughness, it should be noted that the Transpeninsular Line, which follows Line Road (or, more accurately, Line Road follows the Transpeninsular Line), was surveyed in 1750–1751 and marked with wooden posts every mile, and stone monuments every fifth mile. The team started on Fenwick's Island and made their way west. After slogging through the swamp, where they were unable to place a stone monument, they passed by the Bethel site. However, no marker, whether stone or wood, should have been placed there. Even allowing a generous margin of error, the nearest wooden posts should have been placed roughly one-half mile to the east and to the west. A stone monument was placed approximately three and a half miles to the west, and still stands there today, on the property of Line U. M. Church.

Questions about the age of the cemetery aside, it is clear from eyewitness accounts, photographs of the roofed graves, and aerial photographs of the entire site, that the area between the present church and Line Road, which contains the oldest surviving headstones and is the presumed site of the roofed graves, was at least partially overgrown by the 1930s. This area appears to have been cleared out during the 1980s, and it is likely that any surviving remnants of roofs were removed at that time.

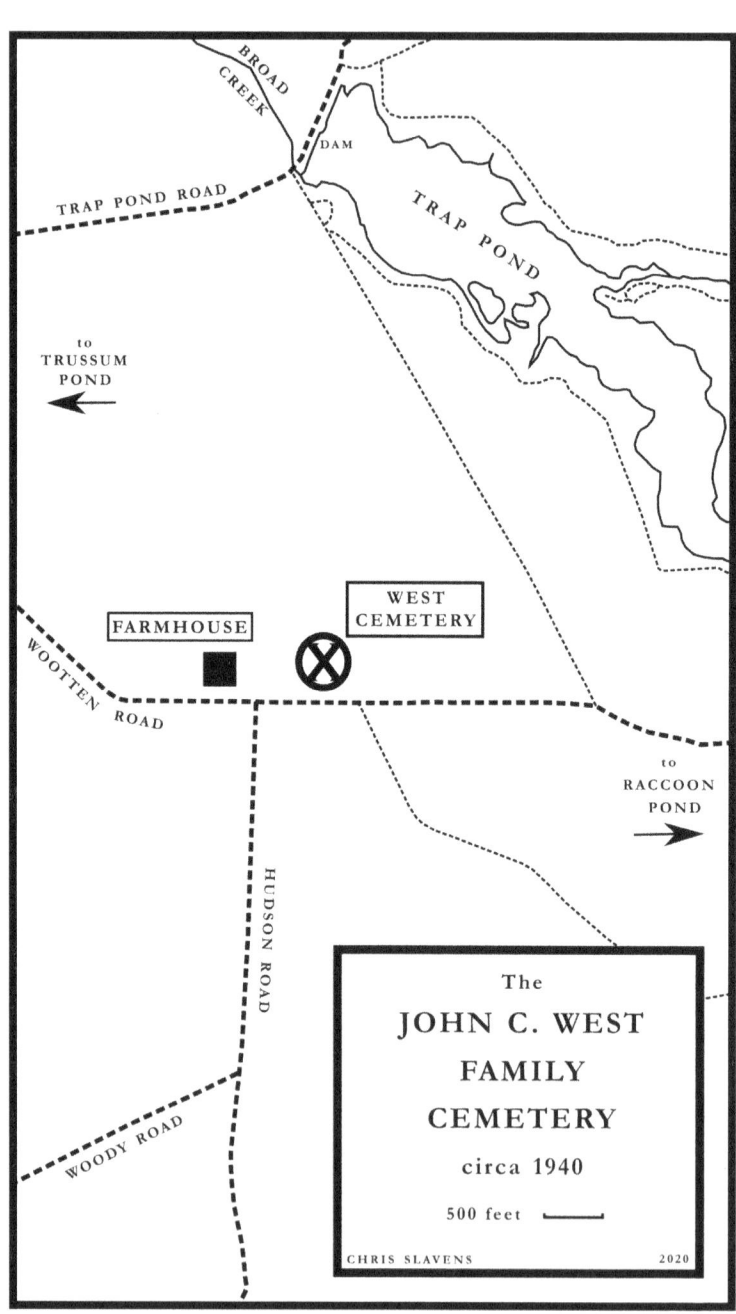

CHAPTER IV

THE WEST CEMETERY & KING'S M. E. CHURCH

When Frank R. Zebley visited Ira West's farm on the west side of Trap Pond around 1940,[1] the neighborhood was changing. In the 1930s, the federal government purchased farms on both sides of the old millpond and created recreation areas for picnickers, while removing stumps from the pond and rebuilding the dam. Farmhouses and other structures were demolished, and pine trees were planted in the surrounding fields. Old public roads—some dating back to the colonial era—became hiking trails. Eventually the State of Delaware would take over the site and establish Trap Pond State Park.

But the West family did not sell their farm, which had been in the family for several generations, and in a small graveyard near the edge of the property, Zebley found roofed graves with headstones dating back to the 1850s.

> ... in the private graveyard on the farm of Ira West, near Trussum Pond, there are several graves over which roofs have been built and each one of these graves has both a headstone and a footstone. The most recent of these were over the graves of John C. West who died in 1858 and Mahala West who died in 1852.[2]

This small family cemetery is notable for having been documented several times. It was included in the Hudson survey in the 1920s, which reported headstones for Mahala West (died 1852), John C. West (died 1858), Maggie A. King (died 1876), and William B. West (died 1878).[3] This would seem to contradict Zebley's statement that the graves of Mahala and John were the "most recent" of the "several" roofed graves featuring headstones at the site.

The cemetery was surveyed by archaeologist Edward Otter in 2008, prior to the development of the land. Otter produced a short report about the cemetery's history and features, and noted the same four graves recorded in previous surveys, but also discovered a previously undocumented burial vault on the south side of the cemetery, just outside the fence which surrounds it. He also found evidence of an older fence encompassing a larger area, including the vault.[4] The identity of the deceased in this unmarked grave is unknown; possibly James West, John's father, as the location of his grave is unknown, or another family member. Perhaps it was originally marked only with a roof or other wooden marker.

The site was documented yet again in *Cemeteries Around Laurel, Delaware: Volume I*, written by Doug Breen and Chuck Swift and published by the Laurel Historical Society in 2011.[5]

The West Cemetery, or the John C. West Family Cemetery, as it is sometimes called, is located on land that was owned by Jehu West prior to 1822, probably as early as the 1790s.[6]

In 1822, Jehu sold large adjacent parcels to sons James[7] and Isaac.[8] James willed his parcel to his wife, Peggy, in 1849, specifying that the land would pass to his grandson, James A. West, after her death, or to another grandson, William J. West, in the event of his brother's death. James also willed land in Broad Creek Hundred to his son, John C. West.[9] However, when John's wife, Mahala, died in 1852, she was buried on James's land. Although John subsequently married Mary A. Messick in 1853, he followed his first wife into an early grave in 1858, and was buried with alongside her.

The third marked grave in the cemetery is that of John and Mahala's daughter Margaret (or Maggie), also known as Priscilla M. A. West. She married George E. King in 1868, but died in 1876 and was buried with her parents. The fourth and last marked grave is that of William B. West, who died in 1878. His birthdate is not given, but West family researchers have identified him as the infant son of James A. West.

It is interesting—but perhaps a coincidence—that all of the four marked graves in the West Cemetery belong to individuals who died before their time. It is also interesting—but probably not a coincidence—that the site has several genealogical connections to the nearby King's church site.

King's Methodist Episcopal Church

King's United Methodist Church, formerly King's Methodist Episcopal Church, is located on Gordy Road near Trussum Pond, southeast of Laurel. Unlike the church at Bethel, its history was included in Scharf's *History of Delaware*:

> *In 1842 a society of Methodists was formed by Rev. James Hargis, in an old dwelling-house belonging to*

William C. King, situated on the opposite side of the road, from the present residence of Wm. F. King and about half a mile south of King's Church. The members of the first class held in the old house, were John and Amelia Wootten, Elijah and Mary Williams, William and Elizabeth Gordy, Alaphare Williams, Sarah King, Sarah I. Wootten, Thomas and Elizabeth Adams, Susan Elliott and several children of Elijah Williams. Money and materials were contributed for the erection of a church which was completed the same year, and named Hepburn, after a Philadelphia man of that name, who promised twenty dollars towards paying for the church, provided it was so called. It stood in the woods twelve or fifteen feet from the county road, and was not plastered on the inside until 1848. Services were held in this building until 1885. In 1881 an effort was made to erect a new church, but nothing was accomplished until 1884, when a

King's M. E. Church, photographed by Frank R. Zebley in 1936. *Courtesy of the Delaware Public Archives.*

building committee was appointed. They decided to build a church thirty by forty feet with a recess pulpit . . . The people objected to the name Hepburn, and by a vote of the congregation taken the day before the dedication, it was decided to call the new church King's.[10]

Zebley's history of the church agrees with Scharf's, and may have used it as a source:

King's Methodist Church (M.E.) is located three and one-quarter miles east of Bacons. It was founded in 1842 when the first church was built. The half-acre church site was donated by Wm. King on Aug. 12, 1842. It was first called "Oak Grove," then called "Hepburn" after which the name "King's" was adopted. The original building was not plastered until 1848. A new church was built in 1884. The dedication services were held on Jan. 25,

The last surviving roof at King's, photographed by Frank R. Zebley in 1941. *Courtesy of the Delaware Public Archives.*

1885, by the Revs. E. L. Hubbard and I. T. Fosnocht. More land was secured on Nov. 2, 1886 from Wm. F. King. The church was rebuilt in 1925. There is a small graveyard and a social-hall. The tombstones date back to 1857. There is one roofed-over grave.[11]

Zebley photographed the roof at King's, or what was left of it. Although the structure is close to a headstone, a careful examination of the spot reveals that it was actually behind the headstone, which marks an adjacent grave. Today the grave photographed by Zebley is unmarked.

In *Visiting Sussex: Even If You Live Here*, Robinson stated: "Like the Bethel Church, people were buried under cypress-covered graves, with cypress tomb markers. There is still one marker left at King's Church."[12] That wooden marker, a small, uninscribed slab with a rounded top, which could easily be mistaken for a weathered footstone, still stands today. The absence of other wooden markers or any physical evidence of roofed graves suggests that, as at the Bethel site, there are unmarked graves which predate the oldest surviving headstones. However, there is no evidence that any graves predate the original church building erected in 1842.

Interestingly, some of the individuals buried at King's are closely related to those buried in the West Cemetery, including James A. West, his wife Mary E. King, and several of their descendants; as well as Margaret "Maggie" West's husband George E. King, who was buried with his second wife, Abbia or "Ibbie." Although it is not known whether any of their graves featured roofs, it seems likely that the custom was associated with the West family, and perhaps the King family, in this part of Sussex County.

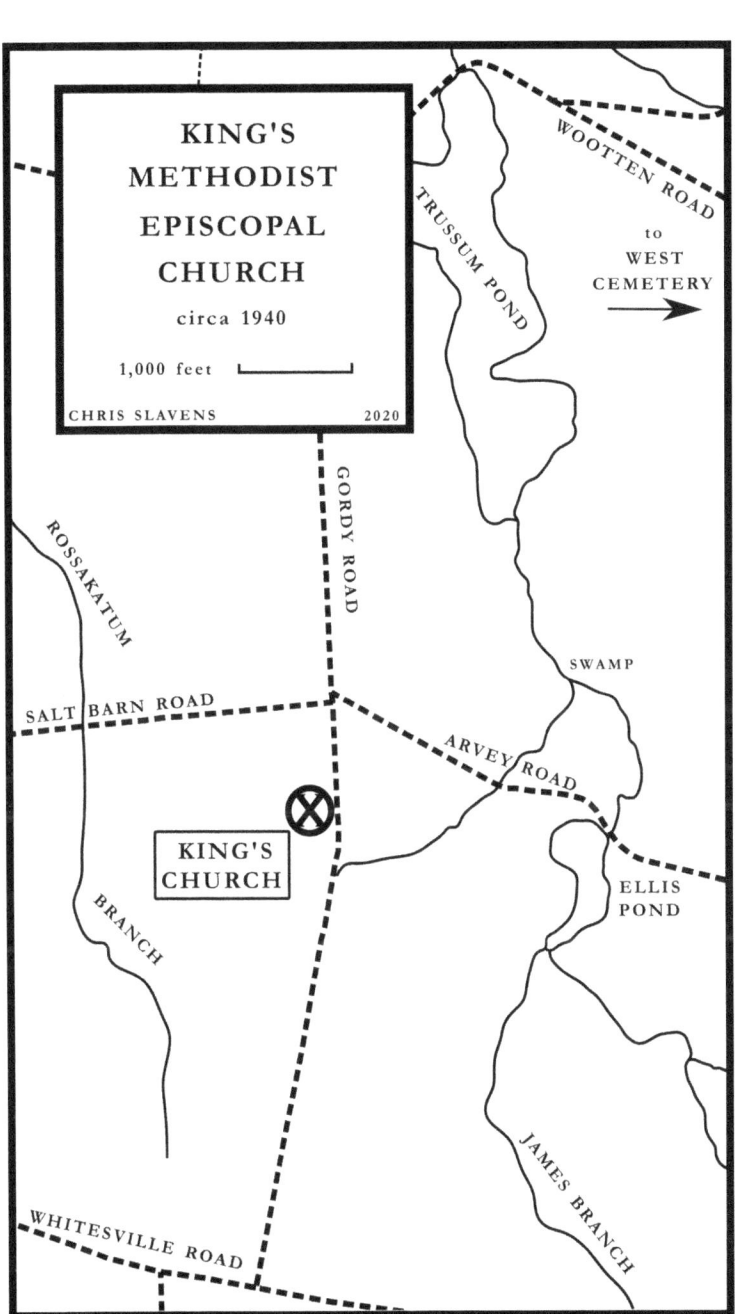

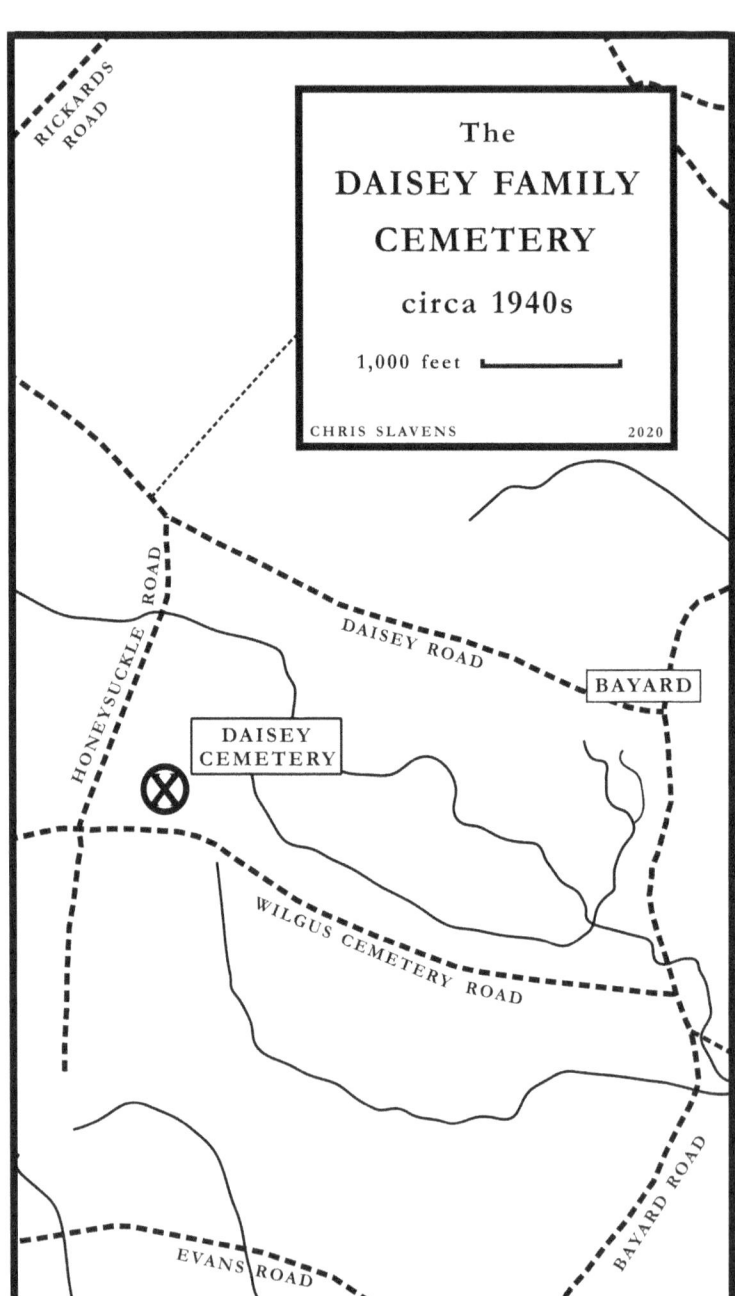

CHAPTER V

THREE MORE SUSSEX CEMETERIES

In *Folklore of Sussex County, Delaware*, Dorothy W. Pepper described a cemetery featuring roofed graves:

> *An old graveyard in back of Millard Johnson's home near Bayard had some graves with a roof on top of each one. The A-shaped roofs were made of cedar shingles pointed on top exactly like a house roof, and each one covered an entire grave. Some were known to exist in the Bethel Methodist Church graveyard south of Gumboro. Few old roofed-over graves remain today in Delaware.*[1]

This site has been identified as the Daisey Cemetery, located near the corner of Wilgus Cemetery Road and Honeysuckle Road, based on census records which state that Johnson lived on the "Roxana Bayard Dirt Road" or Road 381 in the 1930s–1940s, and a historic photograph of one roofed grave in the cemetery.

The grave is that of three-year-old Elijah E. Daisey, the son of John E. and Lucy Daisey, who died in 1891. A photograph taken in 1947 depicts a peaked, shingled roof over his grave.[2] It appears to have been a bit steeper than the roofs Zebley photographed at the Bethel site. Although the subject of the photograph seems to have been in good condition at the time, no trace of it remains today, and the grave has been covered with a concrete slab. Elijah's parents were buried at Mariner's Bethel Methodist Episcopal Church in nearby Ocean View, but his great-grandfather, John Dazey (1790–1862) is buried in the Daisey Cemetery. The grave of John's wife, Hannah Richards, who died in 1850, is the earliest marked grave in the cemetery. Other early graves include those of Tobitha Daisey (1851), Elizabeth Lynch (1858), George and Hannah Holloway (1863), and Janie M. Dasey (1869).

Roofed grave in the Daisey family cemetery near Bayard, Delaware, photographed in 1947. *Courtesy of Kathy McGill.*

The Pomeroy & Beers Atlas of 1868 indicates that the section of Wilgus Cemetery Road adjacent to the cemetery did not exist at that time; instead, the road turned north and followed what is now Honeysuckle Road. The nearest houses on the atlas are labeled Mrs. H. Daisy and J. Evans.[3] The early history of the site is hazy, but members of the Dazey/Dasey/Daisey family lived in Baltimore Hundred as early as 1728, when a 100-acre tract named "Little Worth," vaguely described as being located "back in ye woods between ye Indian River & St. Martins River," was patented to Thomas Dasey.[4]

Dorothy Pepper's brief description of the cemetery, published in 1976, implies that there were no roofs there at that time.

Timmons Family Cemetery

Recent inquiries about the roofed grave custom turned up an unexpected clue when Laurel resident Kendal Jones recalled having seen a couple of roofs at a Timmons family plot below Lowe's Crossroads in the early to mid-1930s.[5] They were located near the grave of his grandmother, and he assumed they marked the graves of children due to their small size. He said the roofs were "up a few inches" on "stanchions" or posts, not flat on the ground. These graves had no other markers, despite the fact that some of the other graves in the cemetery featured stone markers.

When Jones returned to the site as a young man with his father, the roofs were gone, but they found fragments of wood underneath the leaves.

This site is associated with Ezekiel Timmons, whose house was labeled "Z. Timmons" on the Beers Atlas. It is unclear how old the roofed graves were, or how long the site has been used as a cemetery.

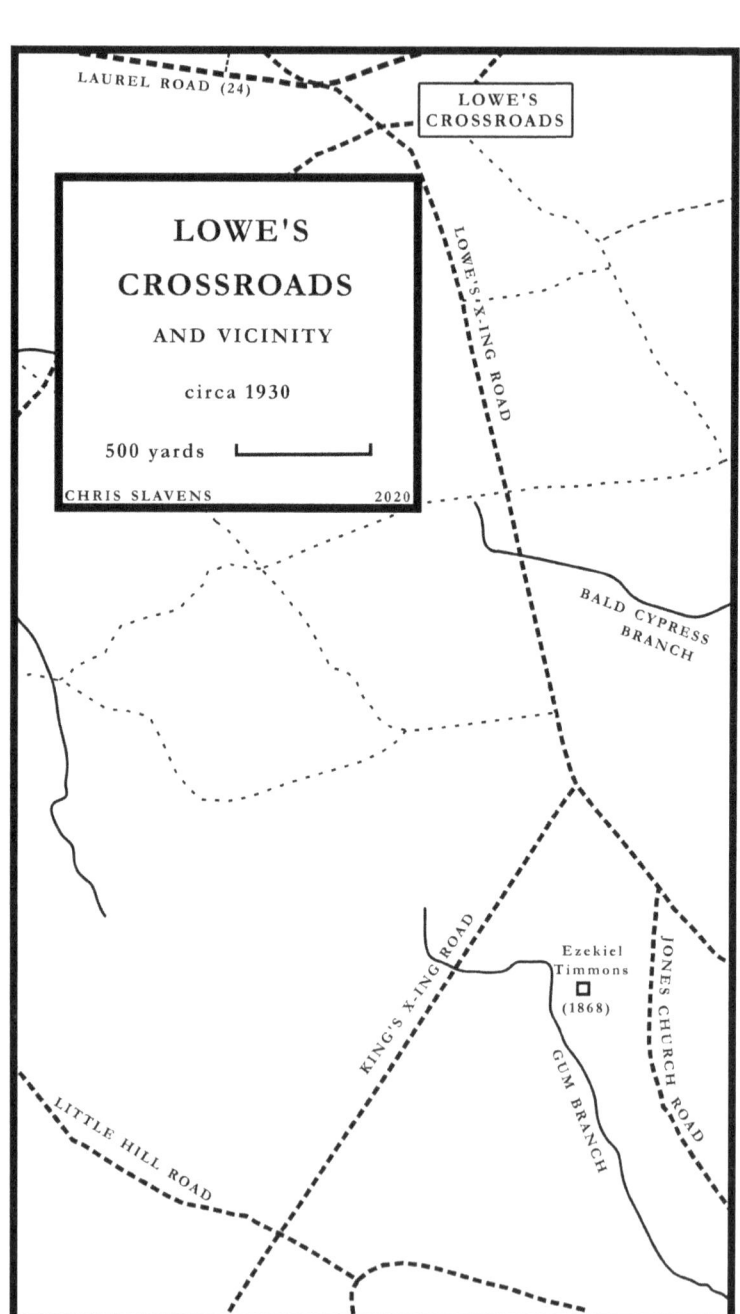

Unidentified Sussex Cemetery

After the publication of the first edition of *The Roofed Graves of Delmarva* in 2020, a father in attendance at a student literacy event at Laurel High School recalled having seen roofed graves while hunting rabbits with his father back in the woods in the general vicinity of English Road years earlier. He was uncertain about the location, but certain about what he had seen.[6] The area in question, north of Lowe's Crossroads and west of Carey's Camp, includes hundreds of acres of state-owned wildlife lands as well as the source of the Pocomoke River. It is likely that the as-of-yet unidentified and unlocated site was a small family plot like the nearby Timmons site.

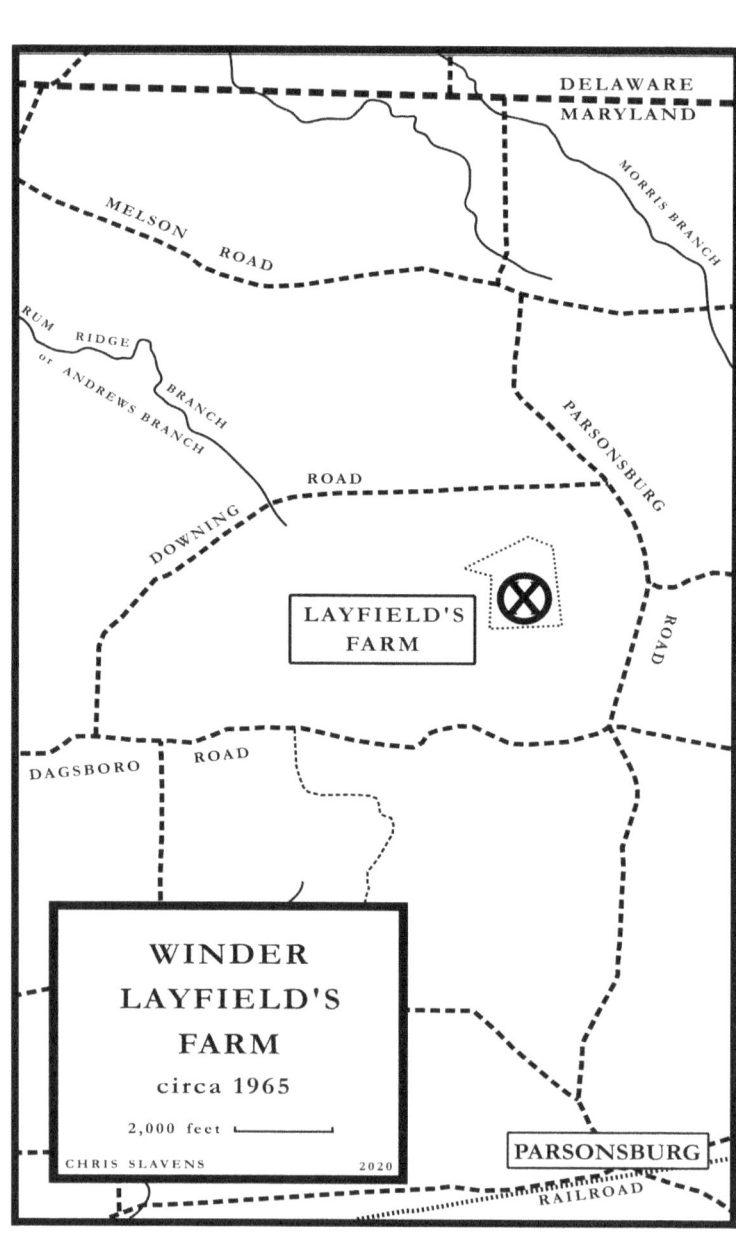

CHAPTER VI

ROOFED GRAVES IN WICOMICO COUNTY

Like Frank R. Zebley decades earlier, John E. Jacob, Jr., was interested in roofed graves and speculated about their origins and purpose. Accompanied by his trusty cocker spaniel, Murphy, the Salisbury attorney visited hundreds of cemeteries in Wicomico County and transcribed more than six thousand headstone inscriptions; the resulting book, *Graveyards and Gravestones of Wicomico*, published in 1971, is a valuable resource for genealogists and local historians.

Jacob was not able to find a roofed grave on his own "until Grant Powell, forester for the E. S. Adkins Co., located three deep in the woods on the Winder Layfield farm off the Mary Downing Road."[1] In a much later article published in 1996, Dick Moore mentioned that Jacob recalled having heard about another roofed grave elsewhere, but no clues about its location were offered.[2]

Winder Layfield's farm

Jacob's photograph of a roofed grave on Winder Layfield's farm is the most recent of the handful of known photographs of the structures, and its subject might have been one of the last surviving examples. Though Jacob reported that roofed graves had once been common in eastern Wicomico, the farm plot is the only specifically identified roofed grave site in that area. Its exact location is unknown, but land records narrow the search down to a 68-acre parcel located south of Downing Road, north of Dagsboro Road, and west of Parsonsburg Road. Layfield inherited the land in question from his father in 1934,[4] but it appears to have been owned by John H. Gordy in 1877. Following Layfield's death in 1981, and his wife's death in 1985, the land was sold to E. S. Adkins & Company.[5] The Salisbury-based property management company still owns the parcel today, and it is possible that some remnants of the roofs, already in poor condition half a century ago, survive somewhere in the woods.

The age of the roofed graves on Layfield's farm is unclear, as are the identities of the deceased. Layfield "said that the graves were those of his grandparents, and that the rotting structures could be 120 years old" (circa 1846). This statement is problematic for a couple of reasons. His paternal grandparents, Ephraim W. and Rachel Layfield, were enumerated in the 1880 census, and although it is unclear when Rachel died, Ephraim received an unusually late patent for an unimproved 17-acre tract named "Luck At Last" in 1893. It is assumed that both he and Rachel died prior to 1900, for neither was enumerated in the census that year. Winder's maternal grandparents, Caldwell W. and Sarah Hastings, are even less likely candidates. They were enumerated in the 1900 census, and were living across the state line in Sussex County. Therefore,

This photograph, taken by John E. Jacob, Jr., on Winder Layfield's farm in the 1960s, is the only known photograph of a roofed grave in Wicomico

all of Layfield's grandparents died decades after the 1840s, well shy of his estimate of 120 years prior to the 1960s. Jacob's book reduces the estimate slightly, simply stating that the roof he photographed "was erected at least a hundred years ago according to information from a member of the family."[6]

Despite the discrepancy between Layfield's estimate of 120 years and his grandparents' actual lifespans, it is nonetheless possible that the graves were those of his relatives.

LOST SITES IN EASTERN WICOMICO

Jacob, like nearly everybody else who wrote about roofed graves, suggested that the custom had once been popular and the structures common. Unlike other writers, he appreciated just how rare the surviving examples were during his lifetime, having personally visited more than six hundred local cemeteries. Even so, he admitted that there could be as many as two hundred unmarked cemeteries in Wicomico County. In 1996, Jim Trader, then-president of the Coalition to Protect Maryland Burial Sites, reported that he had visited five hundred cemeteries in Wicomico, and believed there could be as many as five hundred more.[7]

The vague location of "eastern" Wicomico, presumably meaning the area between Salisbury and the Pocomoke River, fits with what is known about the sites in Sussex County. First, four of the five identified sites in Sussex are located directly north of eastern Wicomico, including the Bethel site (which, indeed, straddles the state line and is technically located in both counties). Second, all of the sites are reasonably close to the once-vast forested swamps surrounding the northern reaches of the Pocomoke. Third, the family of John C. West had roots and relatives in this area as early as the eighteenth century, and the northward expansion of the West family over several generations is typical of local migration patterns of the eighteenth and nineteenth centuries. Depending on how old the roofed grave custom is—see Chapter VII—it may have spread into Sussex from eastern Wicomico.

Roofed Graves in Western Wicomico

In 1996, the *Daily Times* published an article entitled "Search Is On For 'Spirit Houses.'" Parsonsburg native Edward M. Perdue was researching the Perdue and Adkins families, and had sent Dick Moore the following quotation from Steve Adkins, dated 1990:

> *Our ancestors built spirit houses over the graves of the dead. Most graves were close to the front porch of a country home. The older folks would sit on the porch and rock and talk to the dead. (This is true.)*
>
> *The spirit house was for the protection of the grave. Years ago, a wooden box (casket) was built and lined and this is all that was in a grave. Spirit houses kept the rain and snow off.*

The article continues:

> *Steve Adkins thinks they are all gone. About 65 years ago, he saw some and there were a few of the tomb or grave markers still left that were made of wood and carved with names and dates. They had some at a Baptist church on Bradley Road on the way to Riverton.*[8]

In his book *Valley of the Adkins, the Perdue and Other Related Families: Cemetery Records*, Perdue elaborated:

> *They had some of the spirit houses at a Baptist church on Bradley Road on the way to Riverton, close to Dorchester County. These spirit houses had roofs of wood shingles.*[9]

Early twentieth-century topographic maps suggest that this site is located on today's Riverton Road near its intersection with Old Bradley Road, on the outskirts of the community once known as Spring Grove. Unfortunately, not only is the church gone, but so is most of the associated cemetery. In 2019, Sylvia Bradley of the Westside Historical Society reported that a private landowner cleared most of the old graveyard and built a house on the site. She recalled having heard about roofed graves, but had never seen one.[10]

The Riverton site is a geographical outlier in relation to the other known sites, raising questions about the true range of the roofed grave custom.

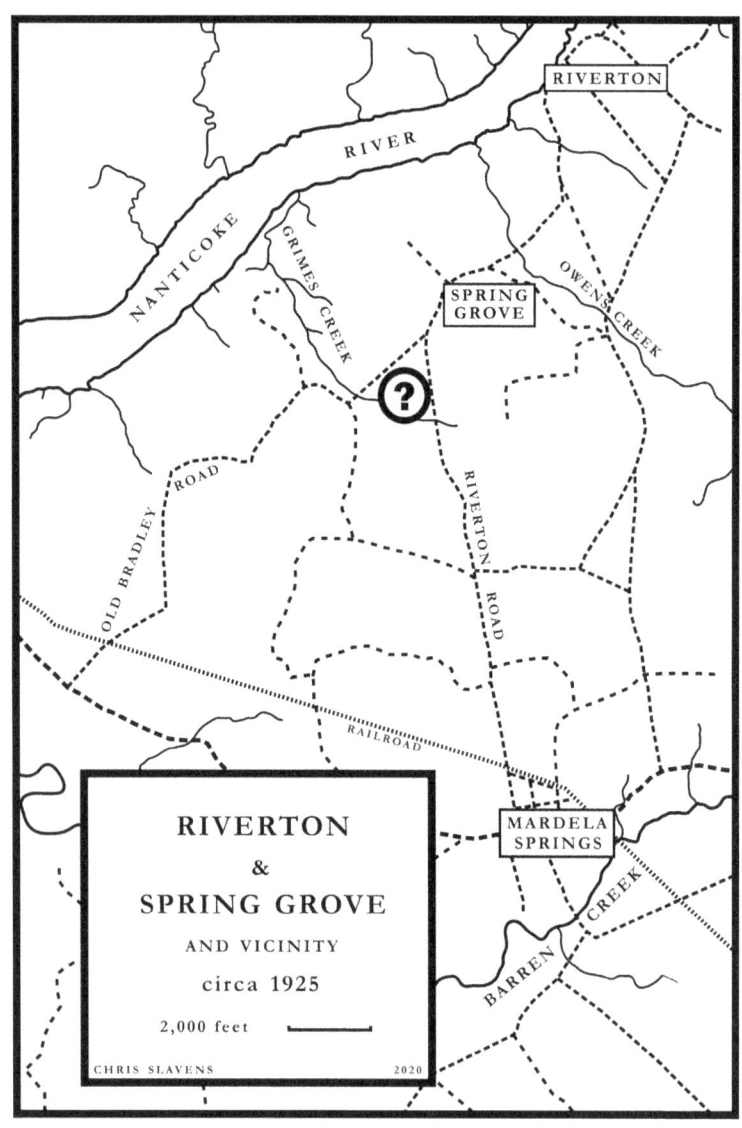

CHAPTER VII

DATING THE ROOFED GRAVE CUSTOM

Dating the physical roofs which survived into the twentieth century, as well as the origins of the custom itself, is important not only for documenting the local custom, but for understanding its possible connections to a variety of similar burial customs observed elsewhere; i.e., the grave shelters and comb graves of the Upland South (see Chapter VIII).

Unfortunately, only five of the local roofs can be dated with certainty, and educated guesses can be made about a few others, but the history of the sites themselves might shed light on when people living on this part of the peninsula began to use them.

DATING THE GRAVES

The earliest identified roofed grave is that of Mahala West, who died in 1852 and was buried in the West Cemetery. The next is that of her husband, John C. West, who died in 1858. Both roofs were still standing when Zebley visited the site in the late 1930s or early 1940s (that is, about seventy-five to ninety years later), although he did not comment on their condition at that time. He stated that there were "several" roofed graves in the cemetery, each with a headstone and footstone, and the Hudson tombstone survey documented only four graves there in the 1920s; therefore, the graves of Maggie A. King and William B. West, who died in 1876 and 1878, respectively, can be assumed to have featured roofs as well.

The roof on the grave of three-year-old Elijah Daisey, who died in 1891, is the latest known example. Photographed in 1947, it seems to have been in excellent condition more than fifty years after its construction, though no trace of it remains today.

Dating the three roofed graves found on Winder Layfield's farm is more difficult due to the absence of headstones and Layfield's problematic statement about them being the graves of his grandparents, yet predating his grandparents' deaths by decades, but a vague window of time can be estimated. Layfield's estimate of 120 years points to 1846; Jacob's slightly modified estimate of more than 100 years, offered in his book in 1971, points to 1870 or earlier; and two of Layfield's grandparents probably died in the 1890s, while the others died after 1900, but probably before 1910. Layfield himself was born in 1892, and it seems doubtful that the roofs could have been built during his adolescence considering his much earlier estimate, so they can be roughly, tentatively dated to the period from the 1840s to the 1890s.

Like the roofs on Layfield's farm in the 1960s, those at Bethel in the 1930s-1940s did not have headstones. Zebley vaguely suggested that they were about a century old, pointing to the late 1830s to early 1840s.

Dating the Sites

Dating the seven known roofed grave sites is more difficult than it might seem, especially considering the conflicting statements about the age of the Bethel site. In the case of the family cemeteries not associated with a documented structure like a church, even if the earliest surviving headstones bear legible dates, it is possible that older stones or wooden markers did not survive. The Lowe's Crossroads site is a perfect, frustrating example; its age is a mystery. One can only speculate as to when the first grave was dug there, or the first roof placed.

The King's church site is the easiest to date. The brief histories of the church agree that the first structure was built in 1842, and there is no reason to believe that any graves predate the church. In the nearby West Cemetery, the earliest headstone is dated 1852, but there is an unmarked burial vault. It could be that of James West, who died in 1853. However, James's father, Jehu, owned the land decades earlier, and the location of his grave is also unknown.

The oldest surviving headstones in the Daisey Cemetery are those of Hannah Richards (1850), Tobitha Daisey (1851), Elizabeth Lynch (1858), and John Dazey (1862).

The plot on Winder Layfield's farm probably dates to the 1840s–1890s, though these figures are questionable. A detailed atlas published in 1877 depicts a house owned by John H. Gordy in approximately the right area; however, the map indicates that Gordy's residence was a different house located roughly a mile to the northwest, on the other side of Downing Road.

Almost nothing is known about the Riverton site, but the Baptist church at the location was probably built after 1877, since it does not appear on the aforementioned atlas of that year. If the lost or destroyed graves date to the 1880s–1890s, which seems likely, then they postdate nearly all of the other known graves. This also suggests that the custom spread to Riverton from the earlier sites to the east.

Perhaps fittingly, it is the Bethel church site, which first excited writers in the 1930s and 1940s, and even made it into the national news, that continues to be the most enigmatic. The initial reports sensationally claimed that the roofs standing at that time were 200 years old, pushing the origins of the cemetery all the way back to the 1730s. Thomas J. Ake reported that the graves were at least 150 years old in 1941, suggesting a date of 1791 or earlier, and Culver reported that the church built there in 1841 actually replaced an earlier house of worship. Zebley contradicted all of these claims by stating that the church built in 1841 was the original, and the roofed graves were about a century old at the time of his visit.

C. Stayton Jones's photograph of roofed graves at Bethel, printed in 1941, seems to show structures relatively free of growth.

Though Zebley is considered a reliable, authoritative source, it might be unwise to dismiss the opinions of long-time local residents like Ake. The idea that the Bethel site was used as a burial ground in the eighteenth century is not impossible, although it lacks supporting evidence. There was English settlement activity in the neighborhood in the mid-eighteenth century, and hills such as the one at the site were prime real estate in comparison with the surrounding low, swampy land, which is farmed successfully today only with the aid of an extensive network of drainage ditches. If some of the early settlers buried their dead at the site long before Bethel M. E. Church was built—which is a big "if"—they probably would not have done so before 1751, when the Transpeninsular Line was surveyed and marked. The 1770s, when the line finally became an official boundary, would be a more logical period in which to expect the use of a site located directly on the line.

However, even these fun, vague speculations are based on the assumption that it was people of European descent who used the site first, and this is not necessarily correct. It might have been an attractive location to the previous inhabitants of the peninsula, too. The fascinating possibility that the roofed grave tradition was inspired by American Indian mortuary customs is explored in depth in Chapter IX.

Dating the Custom

The writers who documented roofed graves in the twentieth century were naturally interested in the custom's origins. How old were the roofs? How long had people been building them? Where did the idea come from? They suggested wildly varying dates—all the way from the 1730s to the 1840s—based mostly on hearsay. Though the earlier dates seem unlikely, it must be remembered that a wooden grave cover built in the eighteenth century almost certainly would not have survived into the twentieth. Since it is impossible to analyze roofs which may have rotted into the soil long before later examples were documented between the 1930s and 1970s, understanding the history of the sites is a critical step towards determining a reasonable estimate of when the custom was initiated.

A conservative interpretation of the available evidence suggests that roofed graves were used within their known range between the 1840s and 1890s, with specific graves dating to 1852, 1858, 1876, 1878, and 1891. The latest grave is both a temporal and geographic outlier, and it is possible that the true heyday of the custom came and went a bit earlier, perhaps between the 1840s and 1870s.

CHAPTER VIII

COMB GRAVES & GRAVE SHELTERS

The roofed graves of Delmarva resemble—and are undoubtedly related to—roofed or roof-like mortuary structures found in Southern cemeteries. Comb graves and grave shelters are found throughout the American South, and have been studied by many researchers, notably Donald B. Ball, Richard C. Finch, John C. Waggoner, Jr., and Terry G. Jordan-Bychkov. A connection between the traditions seems likely, but the nature of that connection is unclear. Are the local roofed graves closely related to the comb graves of the Upland South, which are similar in design but almost always made of stone rather than wood? What about grave shelters consisting of shingled roofs supported by corner posts? Which came first? If they share a common origin, what is the story of their evolution? These questions cannot be answered with certainty, and historians continue to wonder when and why white Americans began to build structures over the graves of their loved ones, but studying the Southern traditions might shed light on the Delmarva tradition, and vice versa.

Comb Graves

Comb graves, also known as tent graves, are roof-like structures similar in design to Delmarva's roofed graves. Richard C. Finch, the authority on comb graves, uses the term to refer to prismatic roof-like grave covers with gabled ends resting directly on the ground, regardless of the materials used in their construction.[1] The majority of combs in the Upland South are made of sandstone, but some are made of metal roofing sheets attached to wooden frames. The latter examples are especially interesting, because they, too, are functional roofs made from typical roofing materials of their time. According to Finch's definition, the Delmarva roofed graves are technically comb graves, and the roofs themselves could be called combs; however, there is no evidence that the term was ever used locally.

More than three thousand comb graves have been documented in Tennessee alone, but they are also found in fewer numbers in Alabama, Arkansas, Kentucky, West Virginia, Mississippi, Louisiana, North Carolina, Oklahoma, and Texas. The earliest inscribed comb is dated 1816 and is found in the Herd-Hurd-Bryant Cemetery in White County, Tennessee. While admitting that some uninscribed combs could be even older, Finch concludes, "Although the earliest comb and its age will probably never be established, it is reasonable to conclude that the comb grave tradition was initiated in the 1815–1820 period, possibly in White Co. where most of the oldest known combs are found, and where the proper sandstone was widely available."[2]

Comb graves in Mt. Gilead Cemetery in White County, Tennessee. *Courtesy of Richard C. Finch.*

Wooden, shingled combs in Mississippi have been reported by two sources, but it is unclear how many existed or whether any survive. In 2010, the late William "Terry" Thornton shared a photograph of metal comb graves in Monroe County, Mississippi, remarking, "Many of the grave shelters remembered from my youth were low and basically of this design—but they had wooden shake shingles on the roof."[3] Thornton was born in 1939, therefore he observed the structures in question in the 1940s or 1950s.

In 1980, the *Greenwood Commonwealth* published an article by Cheerie Sanders about an unusual cemetery, coincidentally named Bethel, in Carroll County, Mississippi:

> . . . *located in the Calvary community of Carroll County*

> near Interstate 55 is a small, well-kept cemetery that is truly distinctive. Bethel Cemetery is peaceful, disturbed only by an occasional passing car, and the chirping of the ever present birds.
>
> Stones in the cemetery reveal dates that go back to the early 1800s, and names that still figure prominently in Carroll County.
>
> What makes this silent country cemetery so interesting is the singular manner in which departed loved ones are revered.
>
> Placed directly over some graves are wooden structures consisting of just a roof gable complete with shingles, approximately 3 to 4 feet in height. Other graves are covered by a shelter about 4 feet by 8 feet in size and 8 feet high. The hipped roof is supported by four columns and the grave itself is enclosed by a picket fence complete with a gate to allow entry into the gravesite.[4]

The cemetery is associated with (again, coincidentally) Bethel Methodist Church, which is located near the intersection of Roads 94 and 95. Unfortunately, the comb-style shelters have not survived, although some of the larger shelters have been refurbished and are in good condition. In early 2018, a caretaker stated that the structures were known as "Victorian grave shelters."[5]

Grave Shelters, Grave Houses, and Grave Sheds

Most Southern grave shelters—also known as grave houses or grave sheds—are similar to the Delmarva roofed graves in that they are wooden and feature cypress or cedar shingles, but there are significant differences. The typical shelter consists of a shingled roof supported by four corner posts, with "walls" of picket fencing or lattice. Some are large enough to cover multiple graves, but most cover only one. Others are more house- or shed-like with solid walls, and may feature a door and windows.

In a study of Louisiana gravehouses published in 1995, Marcy Frantom divided the structures into three periods based on date of construction: Early, 1870s–1890s; Middle, 1900s–1940s; and Late, 1950s–1980s. Each period is characterized by differences in design and decoration; the early examples tend to be "short and small." Frantom states, "The protective function of gravehouses is probably derived from earlier folk memorial forms designed to keep rain out of graves and guard against molestation by animals."[6]

Could wooden combs have been such an earlier form? Or did comb graves and grave shelters evolve from some mysterious ancestral custom?

Grave shelters at Fort Dale Cemetery near Greenville, Alabama. *Historic American Buildings Survey. Courtesy of the Library of Congress.*

Gabled Coffins and Postholes

It should be noted that some of the earliest English burials in the New World made use of coffins with gabled lids. Archaeologist and author Ivor Noël Hume was puzzled when he found coffin nail patterns (that is, nails held in place by the surrounding soil, all of the wood long gone) at Martin's Hundred, an early seventeenth-century settlement along the James River in Virginia, indicating that several coffins featured a seemingly unnecessary row of nails down the center of each lid.[7] The plot thickened when similar patterns were found at Flowerdew Hundred, another early plantation along the James. The answer was found in several seventeenth-century English illustrations of gabled or A-shaped coffins; the mysterious row of nails fastened the two pieces of the lid at its roof-like peak.[8]

In addition to evidence of gable-lidded coffins, another interesting feature was discovered at Flowerdew Hundred, as James Deetz mentioned in his 1993 book *Flowerdew Hundred: The Archaeology of a Virginia Plantation, 1619-1864*:

> . . . the other adult appears to have had some form of elaborate grave marker, indicated by four postholes, two at either end of the grave . . . Perhaps these holes are the remains of wooden head and foot markers, set into the ground on posts.[9]

Could the four posts in question have supported a grave shelter of some design? The possibility is intriguing, but lacks supporting evidence (i.e., an illustration of a European grave shelter from that period). Additionally, a wooden grave shelter should leave behind extra nails for archaeologists to find, although factors such as deliberate removal or repeated plowing could explain their absence.

In 1997, the excavation of an early grave at Jamestown offered even stronger evidence of gabled coffin lids:

> ... the woman's death had occurred probably in the period 1607–10. The woman had been buried in a relatively well-preserved yellow pine coffin. Coffin nails survived, and their positions and a ridge of coffin wood down the center of the burial indicated that the coffin had a gabled lid, a common style for the period.[10]

Another early Jamestown grave contained coffin nail patterns suggestive of a gabled lid. When the early Virginia colonists built gabled coffins, they were continuing a tradition with a long history in Europe. In *The English Way of Death*, Julian Litten refers to an illustration in an early fifteenth-century manuscript:

> ... one sees a magnificent hearse within which lies a palled coffin, presumably raised on stools, with a gabled lid and sides tapering towards the feet. This shape of coffin had been in use throughout western Europe since at least the middle of the fourteenth century, as shown by an illuminated manuscript in the Royal Library, Brussels, depicting the burial of victims of the Great Plague of Tournai in 1349.[11]

Litten goes on to note that this style was modified in the late sixteenth century by angling the sides of the coffin at the shoulders, resulting in a trapezoidal shape. Although the flat-lidded coffin is known to have been used around the same time, the gabled lid remained popular in western Europe until the 1660s to 1670s, when it "gave way to the single-break flat-lidded type, shaped at the shoulders."[12]

Gabled coffins in an English graveyard. Engraving from *Monarchy or No Monarchy*, 1651.

Even so, the older style was not without its fans in nineteenth-century England, as a strongly opinionated piece published by the Ecclesiological Society in 1850 demonstrates:

> *[The coffin] ought to be gabled; and where money is not an object, double-gabled. But the poor man, we will assume, must be contented with a plain gable; the joining concealed by the upright of the cross that will run from the head to the foot of the coffin; while the arms will branch off over the breast. This cross must be worked with square edges; and may be continued plain to the ends, or may expand after the fashion of a Cross Formye. When it is double gabled, a roll moulding may be added at the pitch of each gable, good and bold, and continued plain to the end.*[13]

Stone grave markers in the form of gabled coffins can be found in some Delmarva cemeteries, notably in the old graveyard at St. Peter's Episcopal Church in Lewes, Delaware. Like ledger stones and box graves, they cover the entire grave. Though they are visually similar to stone comb graves, their design is probably based on the much older gabled coffin. These markers are not believed to be directly related to comb graves or roofed graves despite their similarities.

Gable-lidded coffins, popular in medieval Europe and colonial America, certainly could have inspired the development of roofed or roof-like grave markers such as grave shelters and comb graves—but they are not the only possible explanation.

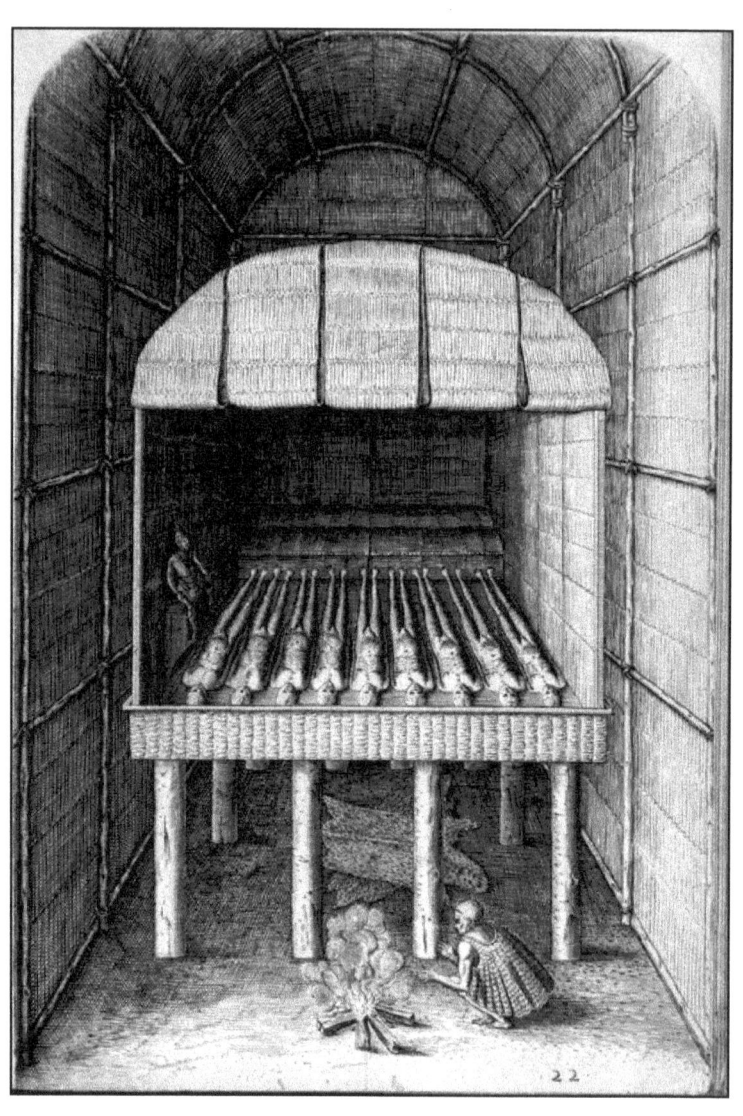

The Tombes of their Werowans or Cheiff Lordes, engraving by Theodor de Bry, 1590, based on watercolor by John White.

CHAPTER XI

AN AMERICAN INDIAN CUSTOM?

Southern grave shelters and comb graves are commonly assumed to be related to American Indian mortuary customs, if not directly inspired by them. It is a matter of fact that many of today's surviving gravehouses are found in Indian cemeteries across North America—literally, from Florida to Alaska—and old photographs, newspaper articles, and other accounts indicate that there were once many more of them.

Though there has been no comprehensive study of Indian gravehouses or mortuary structures, the remarkable similarity of structures built by different tribes in different regions suggests that they are part of a very ancient tradition which we are only beginning to understand.

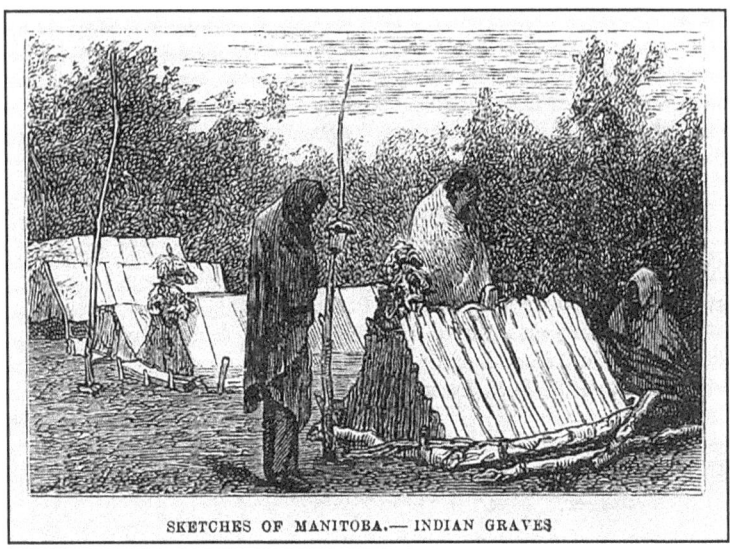

Indian graves in Manitoba, Canada; illustration published in *Frank Leslie's Popular Monthly* in 1878.

Around 1701, John Lawson witnessed the burial customs of a tribe in North Carolina:

When they come to the sepulcre, which is about six feet deep and eight feet long, having at each end, that is, at the head and feet, a lightwood or pitch pine fork driven close down the sides of the grave firmly into the ground; these two forks are to contain a ridge pole, as you shall understand presently, before they lay the corps in the grave, they cover the bottom two or three times over with bark of trees, then they let down the corps with two belts, that the Indians carry their burdens withal, very leisurely upon the said bark; then they lay over a pole of the same wood in the two forks, and having a great many pieces of pitch pine logs, about two feet and a half long, they stick them in the sides of the grave down each end and near the top thereof, where the other ends lie on the ridge pole, so that they are declining like the roof of a house. These being very thick placed, they cover them many times double with bark, then they throw the earth thereon that came out of the grave, and beat it down very firm; by this means the dead body lies in a vault, nothing touching him; so that when I saw this way of burial I was mightily pleased with it, esteeming it very decent and pretty, as having seen a great many Christians buried without the tenth part of that ceremony and decency. Now, when the flesh is rotted and moulded from the bone, they take up the carcass and clean the bones and joint them together; afterwards they dress them up in pure white dressed deer skins, and lay them amongst their grandees and kings in the quiogozon, which is their royal tomb or burial place of their kings and war captains. This is a very large magnificent cabin, according to their building, which is raised at the public charge of the nation, and maintained in a great deal of form and neatness. About seven feet high is a floor or loft made, on which lie all their princes and great men that have died for several hundred years, all attired in the dress I before told you of. No person is to have his bones lie here, and to be thus dressed, unless he gives a round sum of money to the rulers for admittance... They reverence and adore this quiogozon with all the veneration and respect that is possible for such a people to discharge, and had rather lose all than have any violence or injury offered thereto.[1]

Lawson's account is interesting for two reasons. First, the roof constructed of logs, sticks, and bark over the open grave resembles a comb in two respects: Appearance—a peaked wooden roof with enclosed ends (he did not mention this feature, but it would have been necessary to prevent dirt from falling into the hole) resting on top of an in-ground burial; and purpose—to protect the body from the elements and scavengers. Of course, the roof was then covered with dirt, hiding it completely and creating a sizable mound, but prior to this final step, the grave's visual similarity to a Delmarva roofed grave or Southern comb grave is striking.

Second, the "quiogozon" or quiocosin house is said to be the secondary and final resting place of the remains, provided that the deceased had paid for the privilege. It is unclear what happened if the deceased had not. Perhaps the remains were reinterred in a communal ossuary, or perhaps they were left in the original grave.

A remarkably similar custom was described by Omaha tribe member Francis La Flesche in 1889:

> *The weather is apt to decide the order of proceedings. If a storm threatens the grave is at once closed; but should the day be clear and no prospect of rain, then the corpse remains in full view during the entire ceremonies.*
>
> *The grave is covered in the following manner: A crotched post is thrust firmly into each end of the opening, projecting about two feet above the surface of the ground; a pole is laid in the crotches of these posts, forming a ridgepole; the roof is made by laying closely side by side hardwood sticks, long enough to have one end rest on the ground and the other on the ridgepole. Upon these grass is spread thickly, and lastly earth well tamped, and sod laid on, making a mound four or five feet high. The surroundings are carefully cleared of rubbish and dried grass, so that the grave may be safe from fire.*[2]

Once again, a peaked roof is erected over the grave prior to the creation of an earthen mound over and around it. This buried structure is virtually indistinguishable from a comb grave or roofed grave in terms of shape, size, and purpose—only the materials are different.

The Seminoles of Florida practiced a similar custom, with one important difference, as Clay McCauley reported in 1887:

> . . . *some men had selected a place for the burial and made the grave in this manner: Two palmetto logs of proper size were split. The four pieces were then firmly placed on edge, in the shape of an oblong box, lengthwise east and west. In this box a floor was laid, and over this a blanket was spread. Two men, at next sunrise, carried the body from the camp to the place of burial, the body being suspended at feet, thighs, back and neck from a long pole. The relatives followed. In the grave, which is called "To-hop-ki"—a word used by the Seminole for "stockade," or "fort," also the body was then laid the feet to the east. A blanket was then carefully wrapped around the body. Over this palmetto leaves were placed and the grave was tightly closed by a covering of logs. Above the box a roof was then built. Sticks, in the form of an X, were driven into the earth across the overlying logs; these were connected by a pole, and this structure was covered thickly with palmetto leaves.*[3]

Several post-burial rituals were performed at appropriate times, including the removal of overgrown grass around the grave after about four months, but the Seminoles did not create burial mounds. They simply buried their dead in roofed graves. Presumably the roofs were left to deteriorate naturally over time.

Illustration of a Seminole grave from *The Seminole Indians of Florida* by Clay McCauley, 1887.

While the relevance of accounts from colonial Carolina and nineteenth-century Florida and Nebraska to the Delmarva Peninsula might seem questionable, they demonstrate that widely separated tribes employed roof-like structures in primary burials. In Lawson's detailed account, the primary burial preceded the placement of skeletonized remains in a quiocosin house. This sacred structure was familiar to both Lawson and his readers; John White's famous watercolor of a charnel house near the failed colony of Roanoke dates to the 1580s, and the Jamestown settlers encountered similar structures in the villages along the James River a couple of decades later. These temples, which could be quite large, housed shelf-like compartments supported by wooden posts, containing the elaborately treated remains of chiefs or other important people. The term quiocosin—which is a somewhat arbitrary spelling, since numerous spelling variations appear throughout the early records—is related to Algonquian terms for spirits. Perhaps it is no accident that Indian gravehouses are still widely known as "spirit houses."

As early settlers made their way up the Eastern Shore, they found that the local tribes used quiocosin houses of some form. Possibly the earliest reference to quiocosin houses on Delmarva is found in the description of a 500-acre tract named Quiakeson Neck or Quiankeson Neck, which was surveyed for James Weatherly in 1668 and described as lying on the "south side of Nanticoke River, beginning at a marked pine by a swamp near Indian Quiankeson houses."[4] Weatherly acquired many large tracts around Barren and Rewastico Creeks in the late seventeenth century.

In May of 1686, the "King of Assateague," whose people were living at "Askiminokonson" near Snow Hill at the time, complained to the Maryland authorities

> . . . *against Edward Hamond for that whereas it is a custom among them upon the death of an Indian king to save his bones and make a case with skinns wherein they inclose the bones and fill it up with Ronoke, and other their riches, he the said Hamond about a month since had upon the like occasion of one of their kings dyeing stolen away the skinns and roanoke from the place where he was layd . . .*[5]

Although the English took the complaint seriously enough to investigate, eventually they dismissed it.

A similar incident occurred in Nanticoke territory in 1707, when Samuel Marke, Isaac Mallett, and Joseph Tompson robbed a "Quiacosan house."[6] Although their guilt seems to have been taken for granted, six years later, Nanticoke leaders "Tom Coursey, Pantikas, and Rassekettham" complained that "they had not the satisfaction proposed for the robbery done by the Malletts on their Quankosine house…"[7] "Pantikas" is surely an alternate spelling of Panquash, whose leadership among the Nanticokes spanned several decades, while Rassekettham was probably the leader for which Rossakatum Branch, which flows through Laurel, was named.

Another tract named Quiakeson Neck, this one of 50 acres, was surveyed for Henry Dorman in 1734, and described as being "near the heads of the branches of Wiccomoco River bounded as follows Begining at a marked white oak standing on the North side of the Main Branch of the said Neck about sixty yards from the side of the afsd Branch & near the fork of the afsd neck where a Quiakeson house formerly stood . . ."[8]

A brief reference comes from a land commission held in Dorchester County in 1761, which noted that one of the original Choptank reservation's bounders had been a tree standing in Cuiackason Swamp.[9] A year later, a tract named Boald Cyprus (Bald Cypress) was described as "Beginning at a marked chestnut white oak standing on ye west side of Nassaongo Creek and on a point called the Quaacotion House Point on the south side of the afsd Point near the head of Nassaongo Creek . . ."[10]

The best-known account of a quiocosin house on Delmarva is one of the latest. In a letter to Thomas Jefferson dated September 18, 1797, Cambridge resident Dr. William Vans Murray reported that a remnant of Choptank Indians (whom he called Nanticokes) living at Locust Neck in Dorchester County, Maryland, preserved the remains of a famous chief named Wynicaco in a "Quacasun-house" or "chio-ca-son house."[11] Wynicaco had died decades earlier.[12]

Another late reference appears in Delaware land records. In 1798, a small tract called Quackerson Island was patented to Samuel Tully. Just four years later, Tully sold the tract to Benjamin Dolbee, along with parts of tracts named Cypress

Swamp, Out Lett (or Outlet), and Addition.[13] The "island" in question, which might have been a hill in an otherwise swampy area, was probably located near the intersection of today's Gordon Branch and Route 24, before drainage ditches were dug to dry out the swampy land. This probable location is tantalizing close to a mysterious Nanticoke site known as Wimbesocom. Though its significance to the tribe is unexplained, Wimbesocom was mentioned in many mid-eighteenth century land records, and was selected as a gathering place by several tribes in 1742, when they planned a violent uprising which was discovered by the English and put down before it really started. (That is a story for another book.) It is tempting to imagine that Wimbesocom was a quiocosin house site, but if it was, the fact was never documented.

An especially noteworthy reference is found in the name and description of a 39-acre tract called Quaacosan Ridge, which was surveyed for Isaac Mitchell in 1758 and described as:

> *...being in Worcester County back in the Forrest bounded as follows Beginning at a marked scaley barkt white oak standing near the south end of a ridge known by the name of Quaacoson Ridge & a few miles back in the woods from Pocomake River on the West side thereof thence running South twenty poles thence West sixty six poles thence North thirty poles thence East fifty six poles thence North East forty poles thence East one hundred poles thence South thirty eight poles thence with a right line to the first bounder containing & now laid out for thirty nine acres of land more or less to be holden of the Manor of Worcester . . .*[14]

An 1850 plat of James Whaley's lands[15] shows the location of the tract in relation to neighboring tracts as well as the state line, making it relatively easy to plot its exact location and boundaries on a modern map. Today the land is part of Wicomico County. This site is especially interesting due to its location in northeastern Wicomico, as well as its proximity to the Bethel site.

Incredibly, a corrupted version of the name Quaacosan Ridge has survived to the present, along with a vague, distorted legend about its history. The Quackison or Quakason one-room schoolhouse stood nearby until the 1930s, when it was removed from the site, repurposed as a dwelling, and eventually burned. In 1995, 85-year-old Medford Parker told the *Daily Times* that his deed referred to the wooded site as Quoxen Hill, and recalled:

> *There was an Indian burying ground back there. My grandfather said the old head said there was (once) a tribe of Indians in there. But back in the woods was a big hole where the county hauled sand out . . .*

He continued:

> *I've heard people say there was a lot of stuff around that there Indian graveyard that wasn't right. No, I've never seen nothin', never went through there neither at night, went around (by) the road. I've rabbit hunted and squirreled around them woods since 1929, but I ain't got no business in there at night.*

In the same article, 100-year-old Elsie Baker Short recalled teaching at the school in 1914:

> *There was an Indian hole, where (they said) Indians were buried not far from the school. And the children wanted*

to go down there and play during recess and jump into it just for the fun of it. I told them if they'd be good and not fuss with each other they could go down there and play.[16]

Though the folklore concerning the site makes no mention of mortuary structures, the name Quaacosan Ridge and the persistent legend of an Indian burial ground suggest that there was at least one quiocosin house there in or prior to the 1750s, and the English used the site as a landmark. Eventually the structure(s) disappeared, but the locals never quite forgot the site's significance. It also seems likely that they unearthed skeletal remains at some point.

Despite the number of references to quiocosin houses, there is no known illustration or description of one on the peninsula, and it is only assumed that they resembled those described elsewhere, e.g., North Carolina and Virginia. However, a brief passage written by Scottish missionary David Brainerd, who observed Nanticoke refugees at Juniata on the Susquehanna River in 1745, offers some clues:

> *They don't bury their dead in a common form, but let their flesh consume above ground in close cribs made for that purpose; and at the end of the year, or perhaps sometimes a longer space of time, they take the bones, when the flesh is all consumed, and wash and scrape them, and afterwards bury them with some ceremony.*[17]

It is clear that the early white settlers in the roofed grave range encountered wooden protective structures associated with Indian burials, but it is less clear what those structures looked like. Were they quiocosin houses with shelf-like compartments, or a second class of comb-like structures resembling those observed by Lawson and McCauley? Perhaps both? This

Illustration of Ojibwe graves from *History of the Ojebway Indians* by Peter Jones, 1861.

is only a possibility, but it is one that should not be taken lightly. If there is any truth to it, then the claims that the roofed grave tradition at the Bethel site dates back to the eighteenth century might not be as far-fetched as they seem, and, indeed, the church could have been preceded by a cemetery of sorts, albeit a Native American one. It is also worth noting that the sites of Henry Dorman's tract Quiakeson Neck and Winder Layfield's farm are in roughly the same area, while James Weatherly's tract Quiakeson or Quiankeson Neck was located within a reasonable distance of the Riverton community. Riverton is also notable for being located on or near the site of Puckamee, a seventeenth-century Indian settlement located north of Barren Creek.

One problem with any theory proposing a relationship between roofed graves and Indian mortuary structures is that no roofed graves have been reported in other parts of the peninsula known to have featured quiocosin houses, such as

Dorchester County. However, the fact that European settlers did not adopt or modify an Indian burial custom in some communities does not rule out the possibility that they did in others. In fact, the communities along the upper Pocomoke might have been the most likely of any to adopt peculiar customs, as they were arguably among the most isolated on the peninsula, especially prior to the arrival of the railroad. Though it seems unlikely that even the most isolated, uneducated whites would have considered placing the bodies of their loved ones in above-ground wooden structures, it is easy to imagine some, in the absence of natural stone and in the presence of a thriving timber industry, choosing to mark in-ground burials with wooden shelters, particularly if they had witnessed a similar custom before.

Alternatively, it is also possible that Indian mortuary customs inspired the development of grave shelters and/or comb graves in the South, and the roofed grave custom was brought to the Delmarva Peninsula later.

CHAPTER X

MORE QUESTIONS THAN ANSWERS

The roofed graves of Delmarva are a wonderful enigma. They seem to be related to both Southern comb graves and American Indian customs, but each article about them, while perhaps answering one question or another, raises more questions which are not easily answered.

If the roofed grave custom was as popular as early writers suggested, how many other cemeteries featured the structures?

What is the true roofed grave range? The known sites are located in Sussex and Wicomico counties, but were there others in neighboring counties, perhaps Worcester and Dorchester? What about the lower shore?

Why did some locals believe the custom dated back to the 1700s, when the known history of the sites points to the 1840s? Did they know something we don't?

If wooden roofed graves and stone comb graves are cousins, so to speak, then which came first? There are older surviving comb graves, but is that because the wooden roofs came later, or because earlier wooden roofs deteriorated and vanished?

Did both roofed graves and comb graves evolve from American Indian traditions? If so, where did this process of evolution occur? Were the Delmarva roofed graves preceded by comb-style structures used by the Nanticoke Indians and other local tribes? Or was the roofed grave custom brought here from the South in the nineteenth century? Many scenarios are plausible, but none are proven.

Were the peaked, gabled roofs of comb graves, grave shelters, etc., influenced by the shape of European gable-lidded coffins? If so, how does one account for Indians creating similarly shaped burial structures?

Do any roofed graves survive on the peninsula? If so, how might they affect what we think we know about the custom's age, range, and origins?

It is likely that there is more information about roofed graves and related customs lurking in overlooked sources: A forgotten box of photographs in the attic, an old journal, an obscure local history pamphlet, or even an eyewitness's memory. These mysterious structures stood in Delmarva cemeteries for many decades. Churchgoers walked by them every Sunday, farmers plowed around them, families visited them and left flowers for their deceased loved ones. Perhaps they took them for granted. People do not typically write about or take photographs of everyday objects. Earlier generations were more preoccupied with surviving, working the farm, and raising their families than documenting the minor details of their daily lives to satisfy the curiosity of their distant descendants.

It is only due to the efforts of a handful of people that any information about the roofed grave custom has survived.

During a three-year period of research for this book, only one living person could be found who remembered seeing roofed graves, and in the five years since the publication of the first edition, only one more. How many more eye-witnesses might have been found twenty, thirty, forty, fifty years ago, if only someone had bothered to seek them out? How many more eyewitness descriptions and photographs might exist if a few more people had taken the time to document something as ordinary as burial customs in their community?

The remarkable rediscovery of part of the story of the roofed graves of Delmarva, and the disappointing loss of most of that story, should serve as a reminder to us, the living: There is no better time than the present to write or talk about our lives, to take photographs of people and places (and label them!), to attempt to save some sliver of our experiences for the generations who will come after us, for one day we, too, will rest in peace in the sandy soil of this peninsula, and our cherished traditions and customs will, like our lives, pass away.

NOTES

Chapter I: Roofed Graves in Primary Sources

1. The *Binghamton Press*, "200-Year-Old Cemetery Has Roofed Graves," March 24, 1932.
2. *Every Evening*, "Cypress Roofed Graves," April 13, 1932.
3. Federal Writers Project, *Delaware: A Guide to the First State* (New York: The Viking Press, 1928), 510.
4. Frank R. Zebley, *The Churches of Delaware* (1947), 348-349.
5. Zebley, *The Churches of Delaware*, 344.
6. The *Journal-Every Evening*, "Curious and Forgotten Graves Lure Camera Hobbyist Along Delmarva Peninsula By-Ways," April 19, 1941.
7. Jack Culver, "Peaked Cypress Shingle Crypts Cover Ancient Worcester Graves," The *Journal-Every Evening*, November 11, 1941.
8. Dick Moore, "Who Are These Below? Grave Hunter Collects Names From Old Wicomico Markers," The *Daily Times*,

December 5, 1964.
9. The *Daily Times*, "Quota Club Told About Research On Grave Markers," January 27, 1965.
10. Orlando V. Wootten, "Salisbury Attorney's Hunt For Graves Is Over," The *Daily Times*, March 23, 1966.
11. John E. Jacob, Jr., Graveyards and Gravestones of Wicomico, (The *Salisbury Advertiser*, 1971), 1-2.
12. Dick Carter, personal communication, September 12, 2016.
13. Dorothy W. Pepper, *Folklore of Sussex County, Delaware* (Sussex County Bicentennial Committee, 1976), 86.
14. Joan Howard, personal communication, September 18, 2016; Kathy McGill, personal communication, January 8, 2018.
15. Ned Fowler, personal communication, September 2016; Kendal Jones, personal communication, February 2019.
16. Personal communication, November 2022.

Chapter II: The Roofs

1. In 2018, a Facebook user from the Berlin area claimed to know the locations of surviving roofed graves, but would not share any information about them for fear of drawing unwanted attention to them.
2. Federal Writers Project, *Delaware: A Guide to the First State*, 510.
3. Jacob, *Graveyards and Gravestones of Wicomico*, 1-2.
4. Fanny D. Bergen, W. M. Beauchamp, and W. W. Newell, "Current Superstitions. I. Omens of Death," *The Journal of American Folklore* 2, no. 4 (1889): 12. https://www.jstor.org/stable/533697
5. *The Frank C. Brown Collection of NC Folklore, Vol. VII:*

Popular Beliefs and Superstitions from North Carolina, pt. 2, ed. Newman Ivey White and Wayland D. Hand, (Duke University Press, 1964), 91-97.
6. Mary Fontenot, "Houses Over Graves a Unique Burial Custom," The *Lafayette Sunday Advertiser*, May 25, 1975, quoted in Rocky Sexton, "Don't Let the Rain Fall on My Face: French Louisiana Gravehouses in an Anthropo-Geographical Context," *Material Culture* 23, no. 3 (1991): 31. http://www.jstor.org/stable/29763880.
7. Carl McIntire, "Covered graves disappear from state cemeteries," The *Clarion-Ledger / Jackson Daily News*, July 13, 1986.
8. Jeffrey Banks, personal communication, 2016; Dorothy Murray, personal communication, 2016.

Chapter III: Bethel M. E. Church

1. Jack Culver, "Peaked Cypress Shingle Crypts Cover Ancient Worcester Graves," The *Journal-Every Evening*, November 11, 1941.
2. Zebley, *The Churches of Delaware*, 348-349.
3. The *Journal-Every Evening*, "Curious and Forgotten Graves Lure Camera Hobbyist Along Delmarva Peninsula By-Ways," April 19, 1941.
4. Ancestry.com, Delaware, Land Records, 1677-1947, Sussex, Roll Number 23, 251.
5. Ancestry.com, Delaware, Land Records, 1677-1947, Sussex, Roll Number 23, 219.

Chapter IV: The West Cemetery and King's Church

1. It's unclear when Zebley visited the West Cemetery, but

photographs he took at nearby King's Church are dated 1936 and 1941, according to the Delaware Public Archives.
2. Zebley, *The Churches of Delaware*, 344.
3. Colonial Roots, Hudson & Tatnall's Cemetery Records of Sussex County, Delaware, transcribed by Robert J. Redden, 2005 [CD-ROM].
4. Edward Otter, *Investigation and Delineation of the West Cemetery, Wooten Road, Sussex County, Delaware*, (Edward Otter, Inc., 2008).
5. Doug Breen and Chuck Swift, *Cemeteries Around Laurel, Delaware: Volume I*, (Laurel Historical Society, 2011).
6. No deed of sale to Jehu West has been found, suggesting that he owned the land for some time prior to 1822.
7. Ancestry.com, Delaware, Land Records, 1677-1947, Sussex, Roll Number 16, 207-208.
8. Ancestry.com, Delaware, Land Records, 1677-1947, Sussex, Roll Number 16, 206.
9. Portions of James West's 1849 will have been posted on Ancestry.com by numerous users.
10. J. Thomas Scharf, *History of Delaware, 1609-1888, Vol. II*, (Philadelphia: L. J. Richards & Co., 1888), 1324.
11. Zebley, *The Churches of Delaware*, 344.
12. Robert H. Robinson, *Visiting Sussex: Even If You Live Here*, (Sussex County Bicentennial Committee, 1976), 41.

Chapter V: Three More Sussex Cemeteries

1. Pepper, *Folklore of Sussex County, Delaware*, 86.
2. Joan Howard, personal communication, September 18, 2016 ; Kathy McGill, personal communication, January 8, 2018.
3. Daniel G. Beers, *Atlas of the State of Delaware*, (Philadelphia:

Pomeroy & Beers, 1868), 93.
4. Maryland State Archives, Somerset County Circuit Court, Patented Certificate 1473, MSA S1206-1586. http://www.plats.net
5. Kendal Jones, personal communication, February 2019.
6. Personal communication, November 2022.

Chapter VI: Roofed Graves in Wicomico County

1. Orlando V. Wootten, "Salisbury Attorney's Hunt For Graves Is Over," The *Daily Times*, March 23, 1966.
2. Dick Moore, "Search is on for 'spirit houses,'" The *Daily Times*, December 8, 1996.
3. Archives of Maryland Online, Wicomico County, Deed, digital image, Book 967, 334-335, November 18, 1981. http://www.mdlandrec.net
4. Lake, Griffing, and Stevenson, *Atlas of Wicomico, Somerset & Worcester Cos., Md.*, (1877), 13.
5. Archives of Maryland Online, Wicomico County, Deed, digital image, Book 1079, 292-294, October 7, 1986. http://www.mdlandrec.net
6. Jacob, *Graveyards and Gravestones of Wicomico*, 1.
7. Dick Moore, "Family cemeteries seldom used," The *Daily Times*, January 7, 1966.
8. Dick Moore, "Search is on for 'spirit houses,'" The *Daily Times*, December 8, 1996.
9. Edward M. Perdue, *Valley of the Adkins, the Perdue and Other Related Families: Cemetery Records*, (1995), I-2.
10. Sylvia Bradley, personal communication, February 18, 2019.

Chapter VII: Dating the Roofed Grave Custom

Note: Because Chapter VII consists of an analysis of previously cited facts, I have chosen not to duplicate the notes provided for previous chapters.

Chapter VIII: Comb Graves and Grave Shelters

1. Richard C. Finch, "The Tennessee Comb Grave Tradition," *Tennessee Folklore Society Bulletin*, Vol. LXX, Nos. 1-2, Spring & Fall 2014, (2018): 3.
2. Finch, "The Tennessee Comb Grave Tradition," 29-30.
   Note: The 1816 inscribed comb is reported in an updated edition of Finch's paper "The Tennessee Comb Grave Tradition," which appears online at http://www.grater-utabaga.com.
3. Terry Thornton, "Grave Shelters," Terry Thornton's Hill Country of Monroe County Mississippi, April 9, 2010. http://hillcountryhogsblog.blogspot.com/2010/04/grave-shelters.html
4. Cheerie Sanders, "Peaceful rural cemetery features roofed gravesites," The *Greenwood Commonwealth*, January 20, 1980.
5. Heaven Roberts, personal communication, January 5, 2018.
6. Marcy Frantom, "Gravehouses of North Louisiana: Culture History and Typology," *Material Culture* 27, no. 2 (1995): 21-48. http://www.jstor.org/stable/29763984
7. Ivor Noël Hume, *Martin's Hundred*, (University of Virginia Press, 1991), 38-39.
8. Noël Hume, *Martin's Hundred*, 76-83.
9. James Deetz, *Flowerdew Hundred: The Archaeology of a Virginia Plantation, 1619–1864*, (University of Virginia Press, 1993), 37-38.

10. William M. Kelso, *Jamestown: The Buried Truth*, (University of Virginia Press, 2006), 139.
11. Julian Litten, *The English Way of Death: The Common Funeral Since 1450*, (Robert Hale, 1991), 88-89.
12. Litten, English Way of Death, 90-99.
13. "On Funerals and Cemeteries," *The Ecclesiologist*, Volume X, (1850), 333.

Chapter IX: An American Indian Connection?

1. John Lawson, *The History of Carolina*, (Strother & Marcom, 1860), 296-298.
2. Francis La Flesche, "Death and Funeral Customs among the Omahas," *The Journal of American Folklore* 2, no. 4 (1889): 9. http://www.jstor.org/stable/533695
3. Clay McCauley, "The Seminole Indians of Florida," in *United States Bureau of American Ethnology, Fifth Annual Report, 1883–1884* (Washington, D.C.: Government Printing Office, 1887), 520-522.
4. William B. Marye, "Former Indian Sites in Maryland, as Located by Early Colonial Records," *American Antiquity* 2, no. 1 (1936): 43. http://www.jstor.org/stable/275041
   Note: 1688, not 1668, according to Ruth T. Dryden, *Calvert Papers: Rent Rolls of Somerset County, Maryland, 1663–1723*, 88, 107.
5. *Archives of Maryland: Proceedings of the Council of Maryland, 1667–1687/8*, (Maryland Historical Society, 1887), 480.
6. *Archives of Maryland: Proceedings of the Council of Maryland, 1698–1731*, (Maryland Historical Society, 1905), 215.
7. *Archives of Maryland: Proceedings and Acts of the General Assembly of Maryland, Oct. 25, 1711 – Oct. 9, 1714*, (Maryland Historical Society, 1909), 228-229.

8. Maryland State Archives, Somerset County Circuit Court, Patented Certificate 1981, MSA S1206-2133. http://www.plats.net

9. Marye, "Former Indian Sites in Maryland, as Located by Early Colonial Records," 44.

10. Maryland State Archives, Worcester County Circuit Court, Patented Certificate 330, MSA S1210-364. http://www.plats.net

11. Daniel G. Brinton, "A Vocabulary of the Nanticoke Dialect," *Proceedings of the American Philosophical Society* 31, no. 142 (1893): 325-333. https://www.jstor.org/stable/982971

12. C. A. Weslager, "Wynicaco: A Choptank Indian Chief," *Proceedings of the American Philosophical Society* 87, no. 5 (1944): 398-402. http://www.jstor.org/stable/985292

13. Ancestry.com, Delaware, Land Records, 1677-1947, Sussex, Roll Number 9, 361-362.

14. Maryland State Archives, Worcester County Circuit Court, Patented Certificate 2116, MSA S1210-2261. http://www.plats.net

15. Maryland State Archives, Worcester County Circuit Court, Patented Certificate 2624, MSA S1210-2809 http://www.plats.net

16. Brice Stump, "The good people of Quakason," The *Daily Times*, August 15, 1995.

17. Diary of David Brainerd, quoted in Gary D. Shaffer, "Nanticoke Indian Burial Practices: Challenges for Archaeological Interpretation," *Archaeology of Eastern North America* 33 (2005), 144-145.

ABOUT THE AUTHOR

Christopher Slavens lives in Sussex County, Delaware, with his wife, Crystal. He has contributed to numerous newspapers and publications including the *News Journal* and the *Laurel Star*. In addition to writing, Chris enjoys gardening, hunting, and collecting books. He is also a member of the Archaeological Society of Delaware, and serves on the board of directors of the Laurel Historical Society.

www.ingramcontent.com/pod-product-compliance
Lightning Source LLC
Chambersburg PA
CBHW062027290426
44108CB00025B/2815